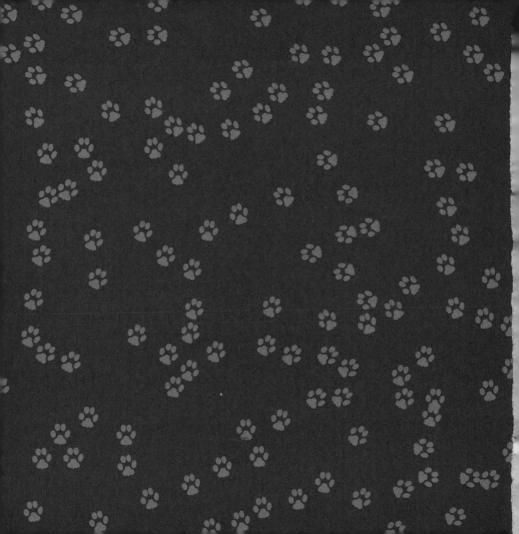

WHEN CATS TURN
TURN
BAD

Kitty Litter

WHEN CATS TURN BAD

Copyright © Summersdale Publishers Ltd, 2009

Text by Sarah Herman

All rights reserved.

No part of this book may be reproduced by any means, nor transmitted, nor translated into a machine language, without the written permission of the publishers.

Condition of Sale
This book is sold subject to the condition that it shall not, by way of trade or otherwise, be lent, re-sold, hired out or otherwise circulated in any form of binding or cover other than that in which it is published and without a similar condition including this condition being imposed on the subsequent publisher.

Summersdale Publishers Ltd
46 West Street
Chichester
West Sussex
PO19 1RP
UK

www.summersdale.com

Printed and bound in China

ISBN: 978-1-84024-784-8

All images © Shutterstock

Substantial discounts on bulk quantities of Summersdale books are available to corporations, professional associations and other organisations. For details telephone Summersdale Publishers on (+44-1243-771107), fax (+44-1243-786300) or email (nicky@summersdale.com).

WHEN CATS TURN BAD

Kitty Litter

summersdale

MEET KITTY LITTER

INTRODUCTION

Cats are badass. Seriously. They may look all fluffy and innocent, with their soft fur and little paws, but behind every pricked ear and twitching tail is a pro at trashing curtains, tearing up the lawn. It might seem like all they do is sleep, eat and skulk around the place, but these feisty fellows have nine lives for a reason. Whether they're experimenting with the latest club drugs or checking out rival cliques' territory, it's most pussies are just looking for kicks.

If your cat comes down on your garden lily borders and got the munchies, if he's fighting with next door's dog he's using language that would make you blush, and if he's running up against anyone the chances are they're out to get some action. These pages take you to the darker side of kittydom through the mischievous minds of some very naughty cats. Prepare yourself, cat lover, because this is what happens when cats turn bad…

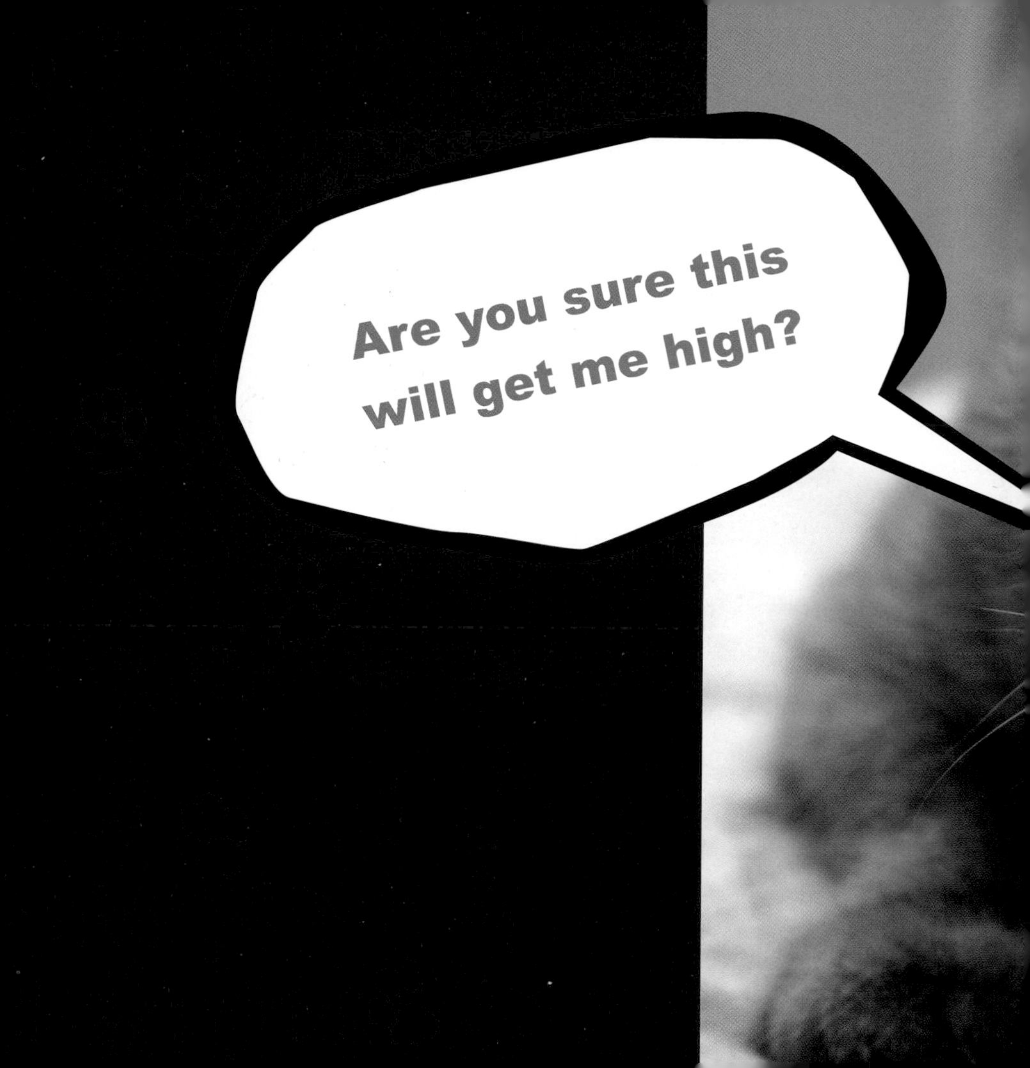
Are you sure this will get me high?

Would you mind helping me? It would appear my giant penis is lodged in between these branches.

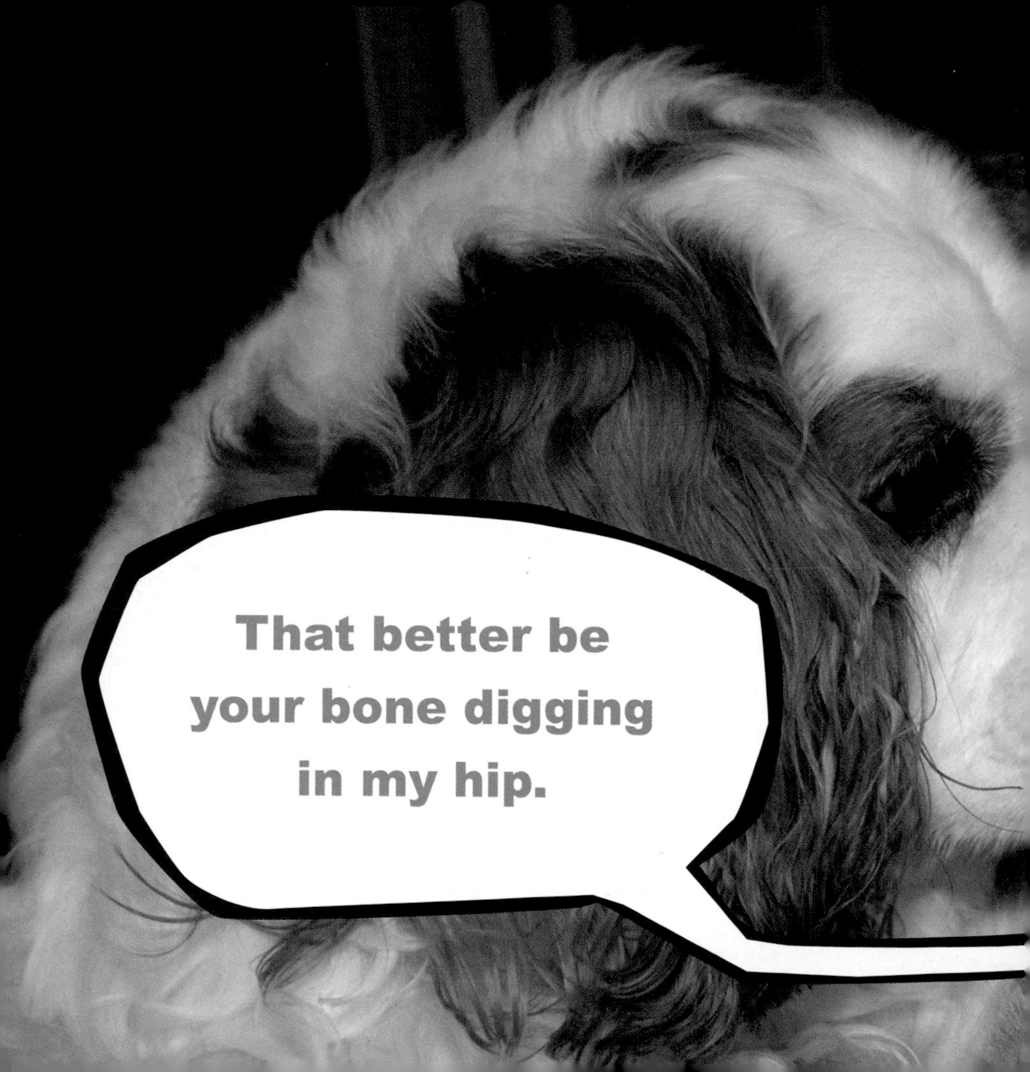
That better be your bone digging in my hip.

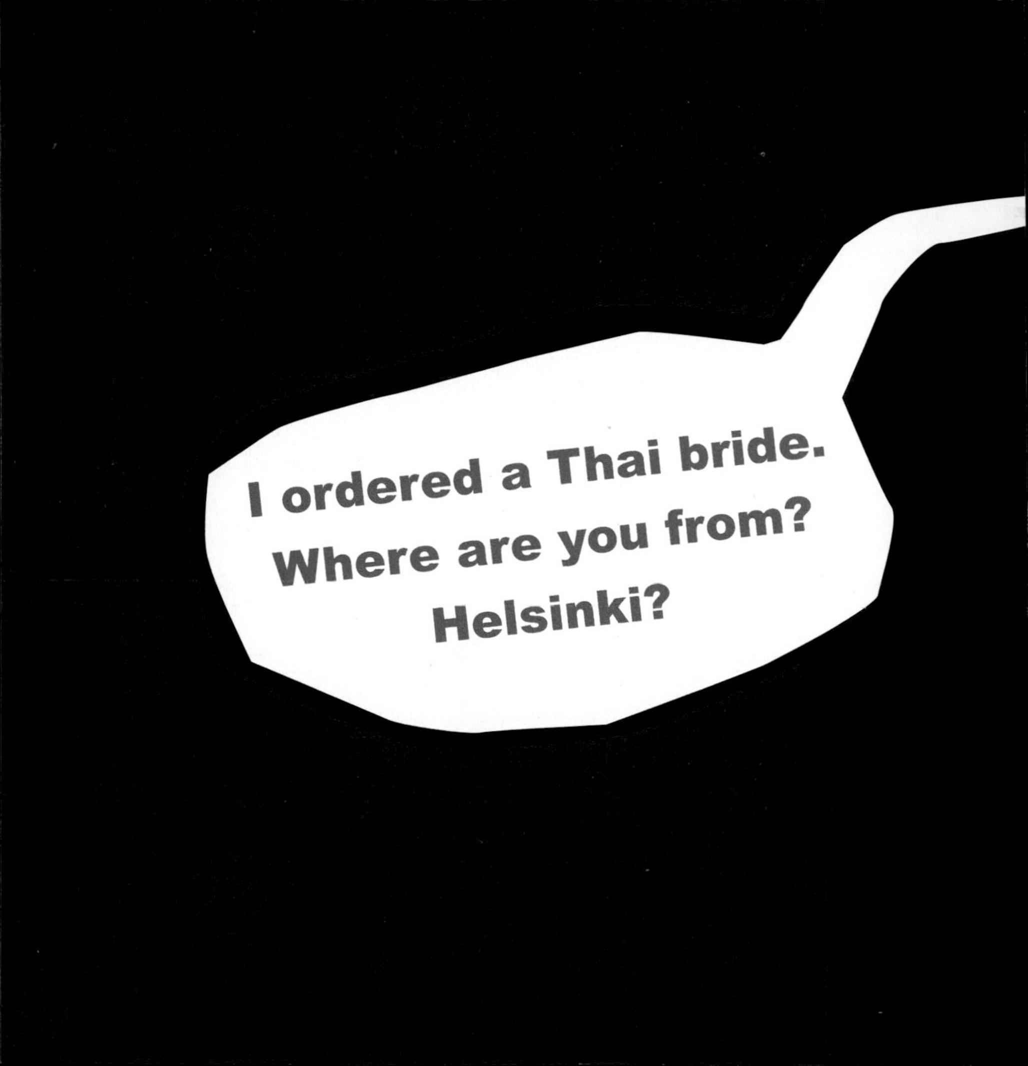
I ordered a Thai bride. Where are you from? Helsinki?

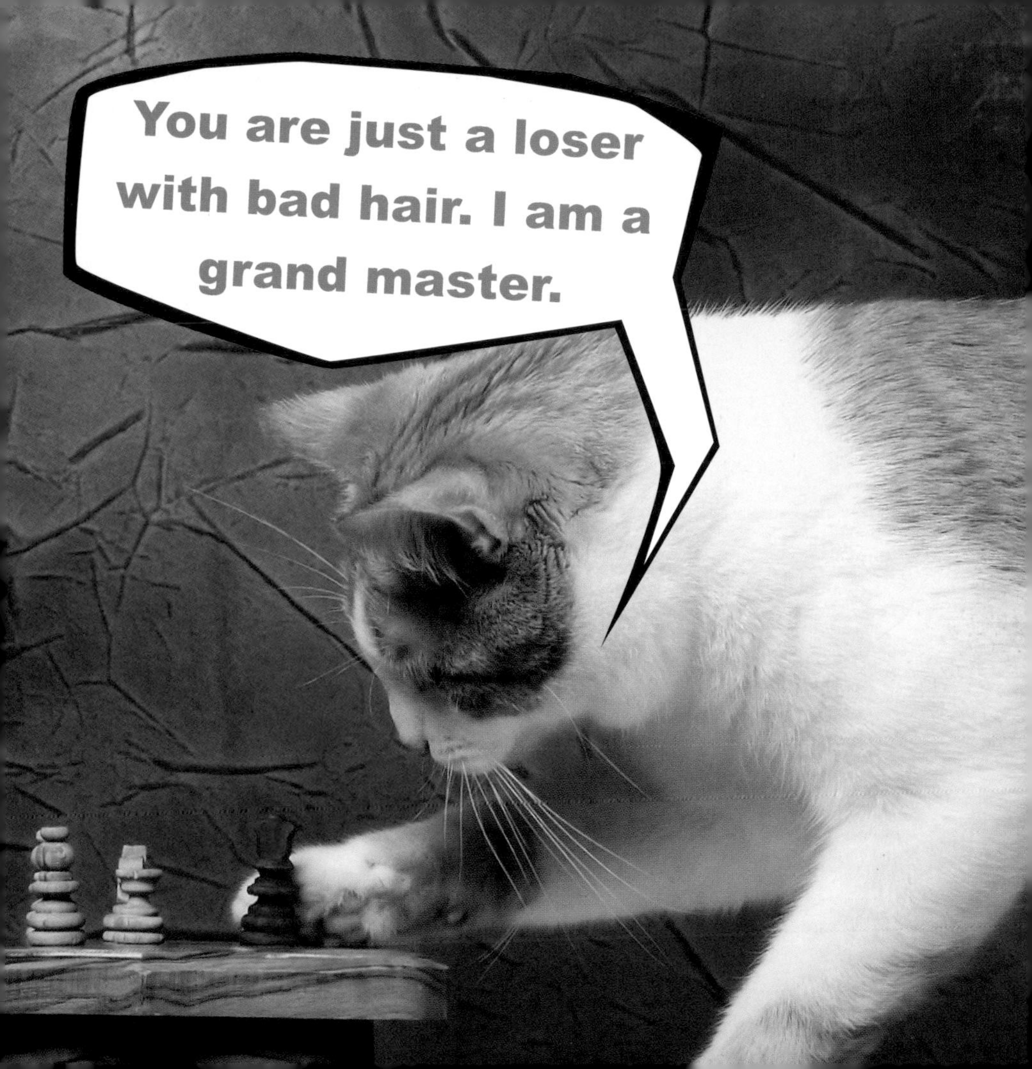
You are just a loser with bad hair. I am a grand master.

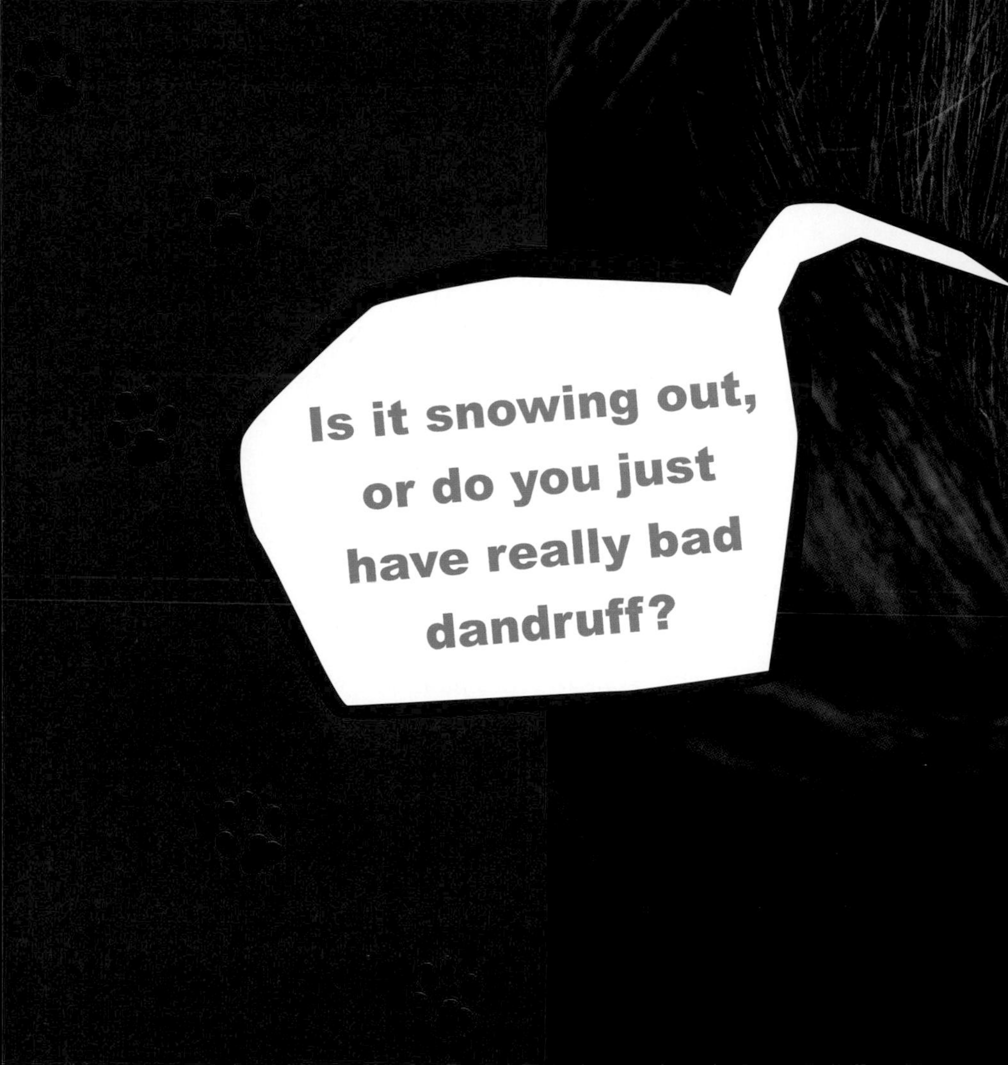
Is it snowing out, or do you just have really bad dandruff?

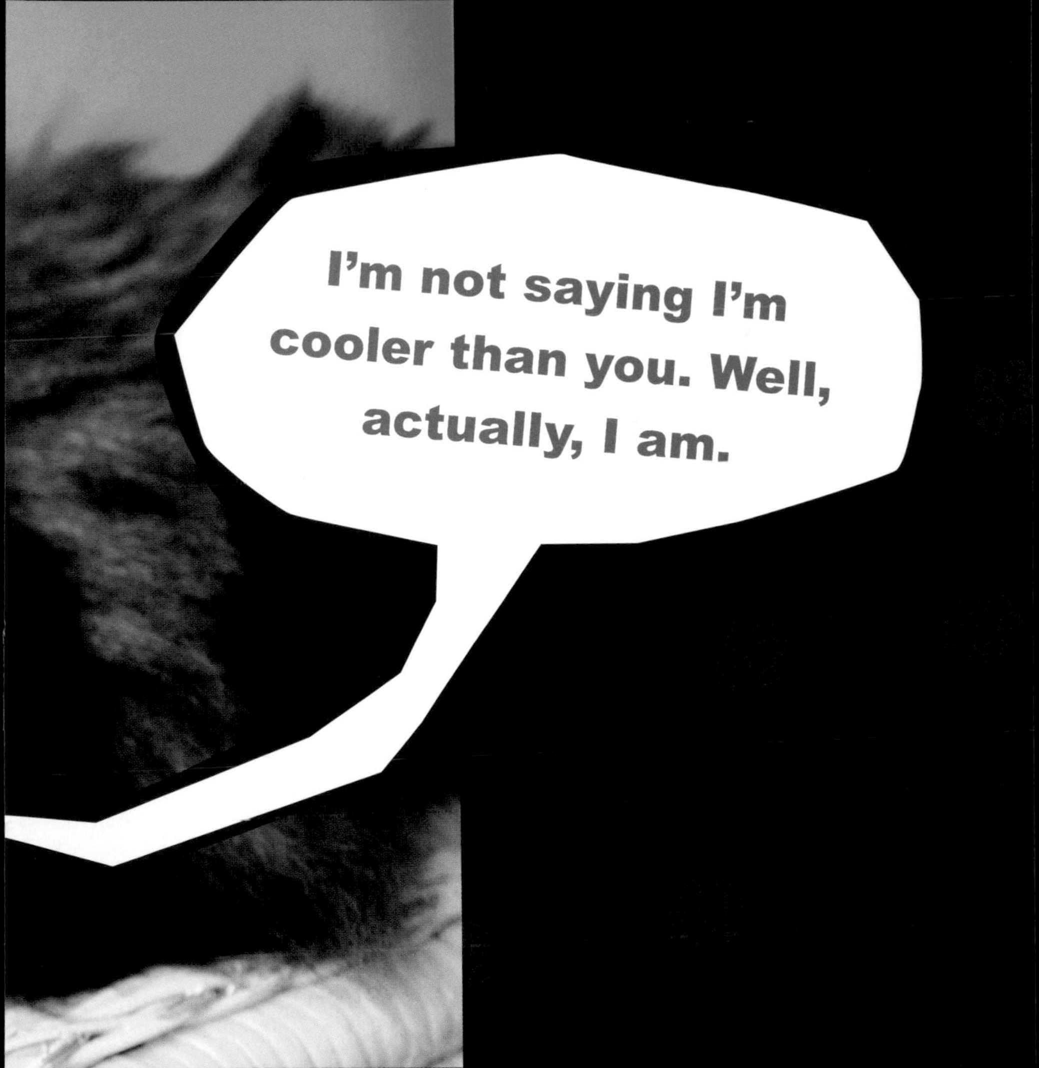
I'm not saying I'm cooler than you. Well, actually, I am.

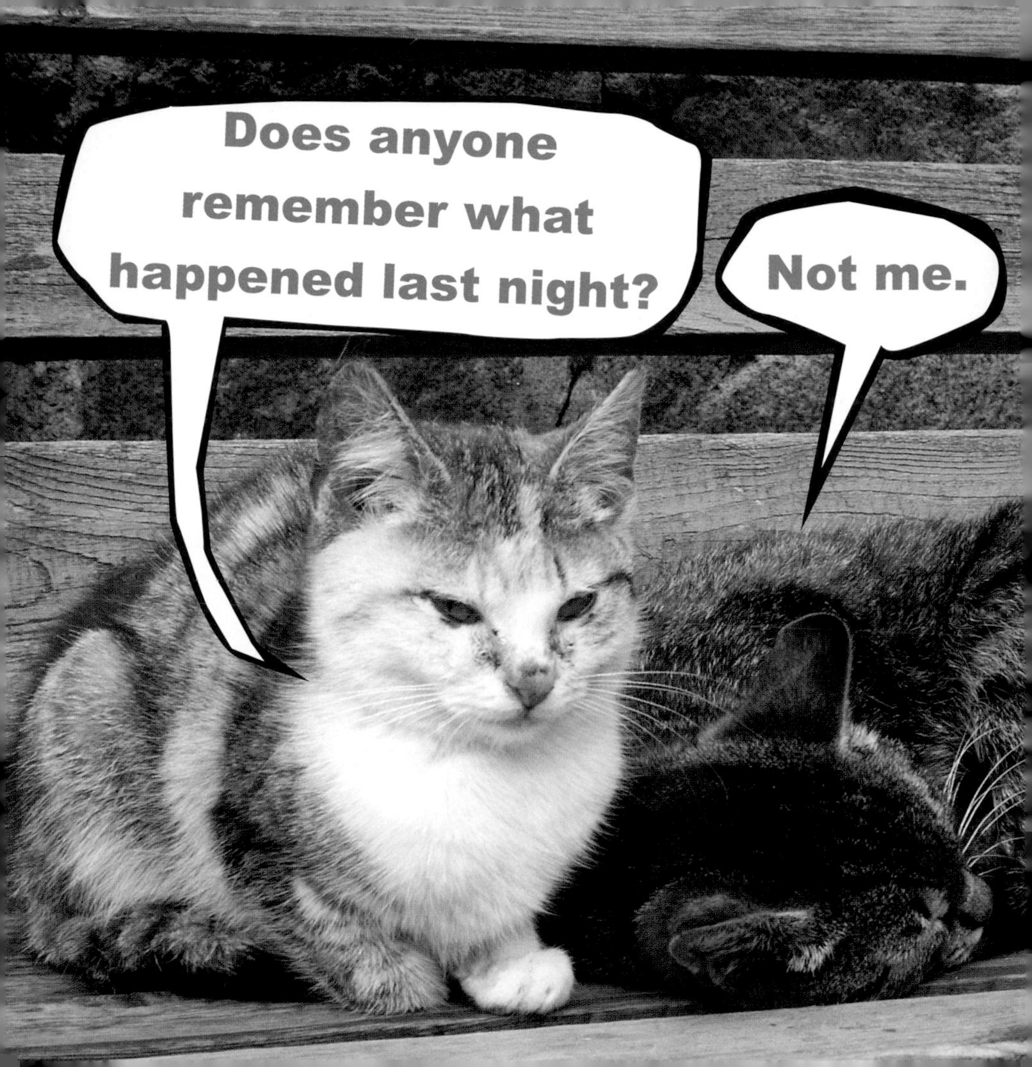
Does anyone remember what happened last night?
Not me.

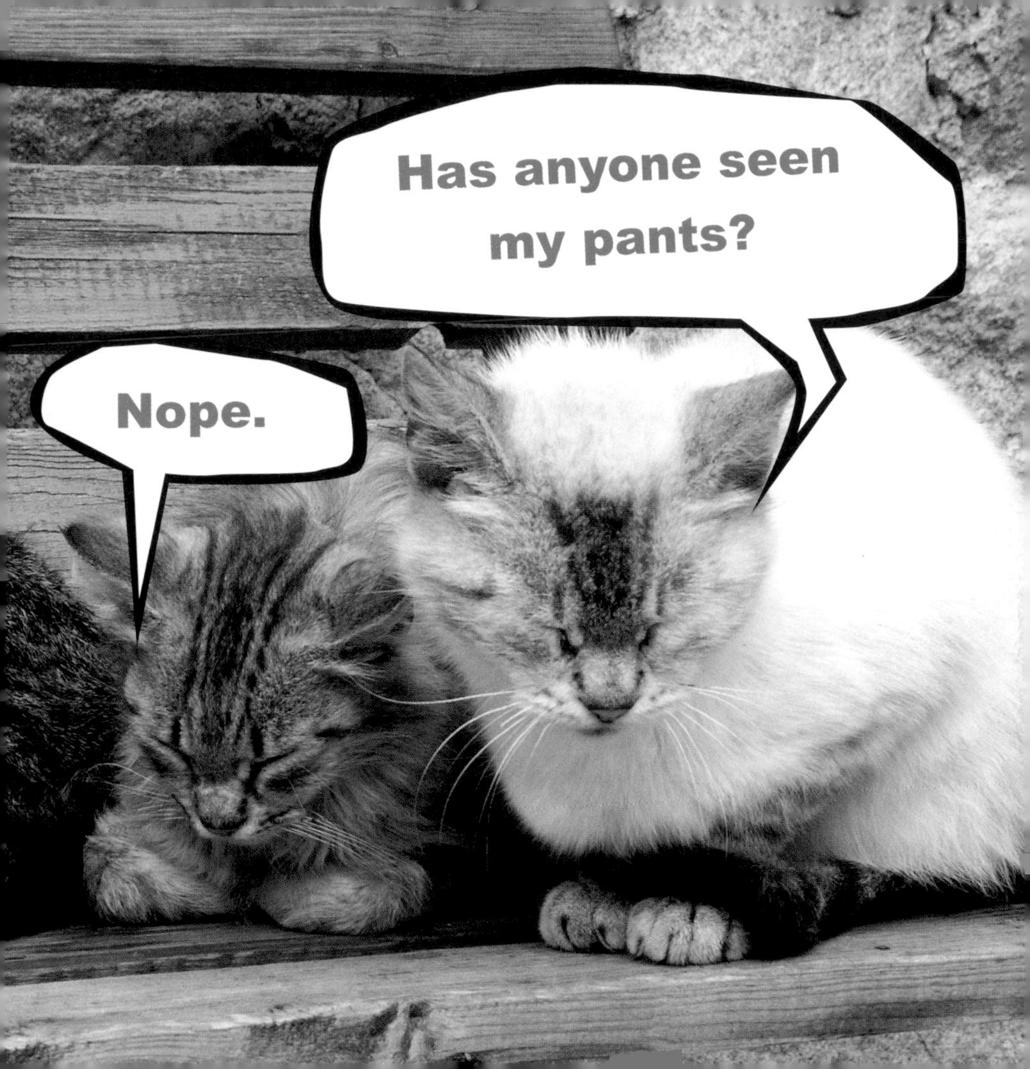
Has anyone seen my pants?
Nope.

Did you just fart?

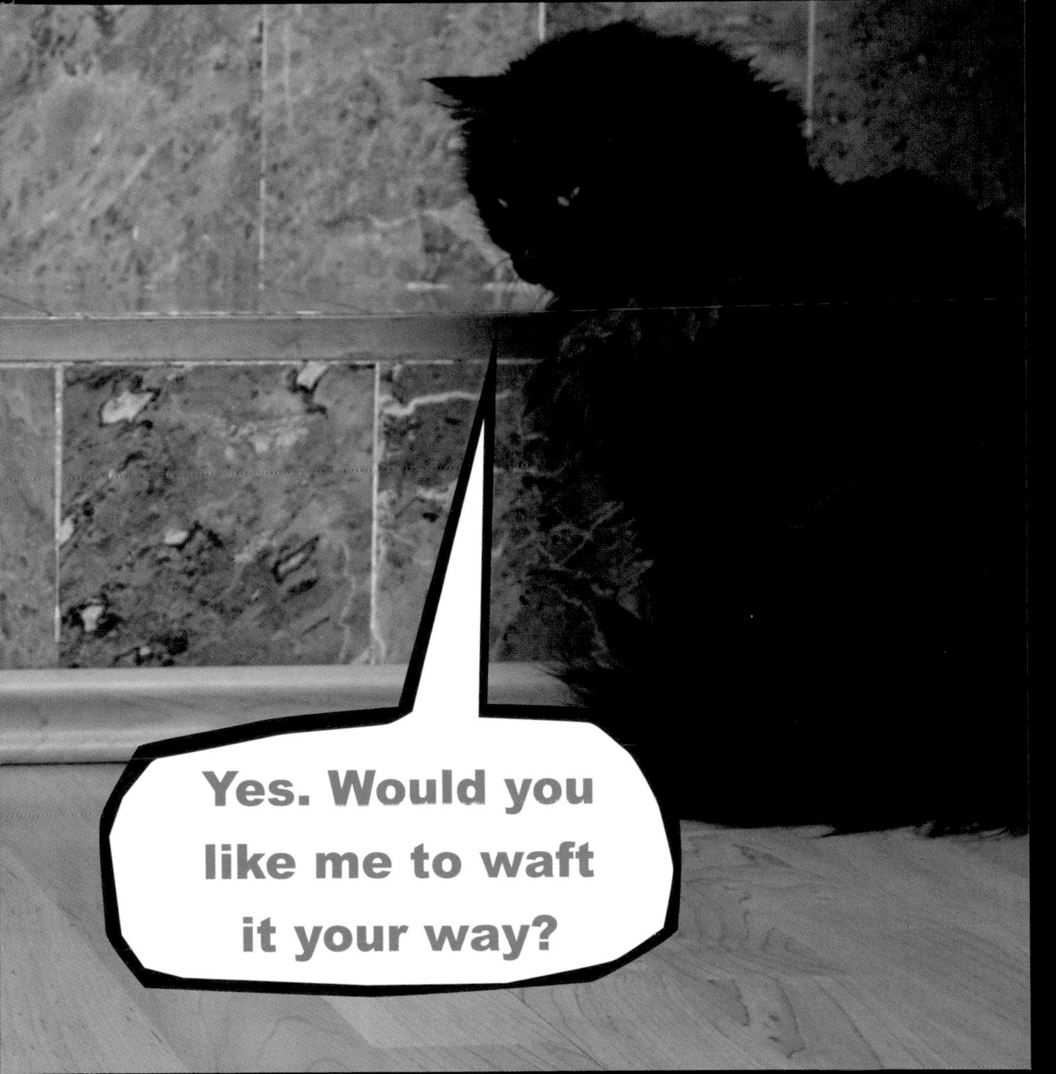
Yes. Would you like me to waft it your way?

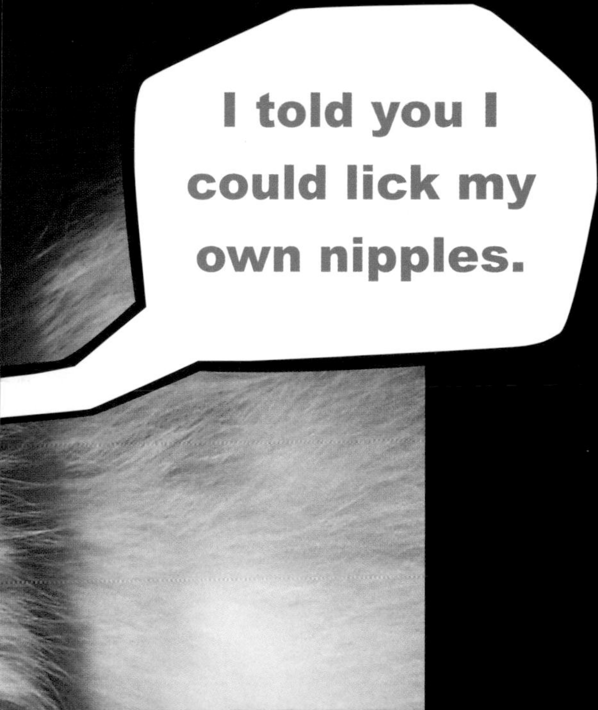
I told you I could lick my own nipples.

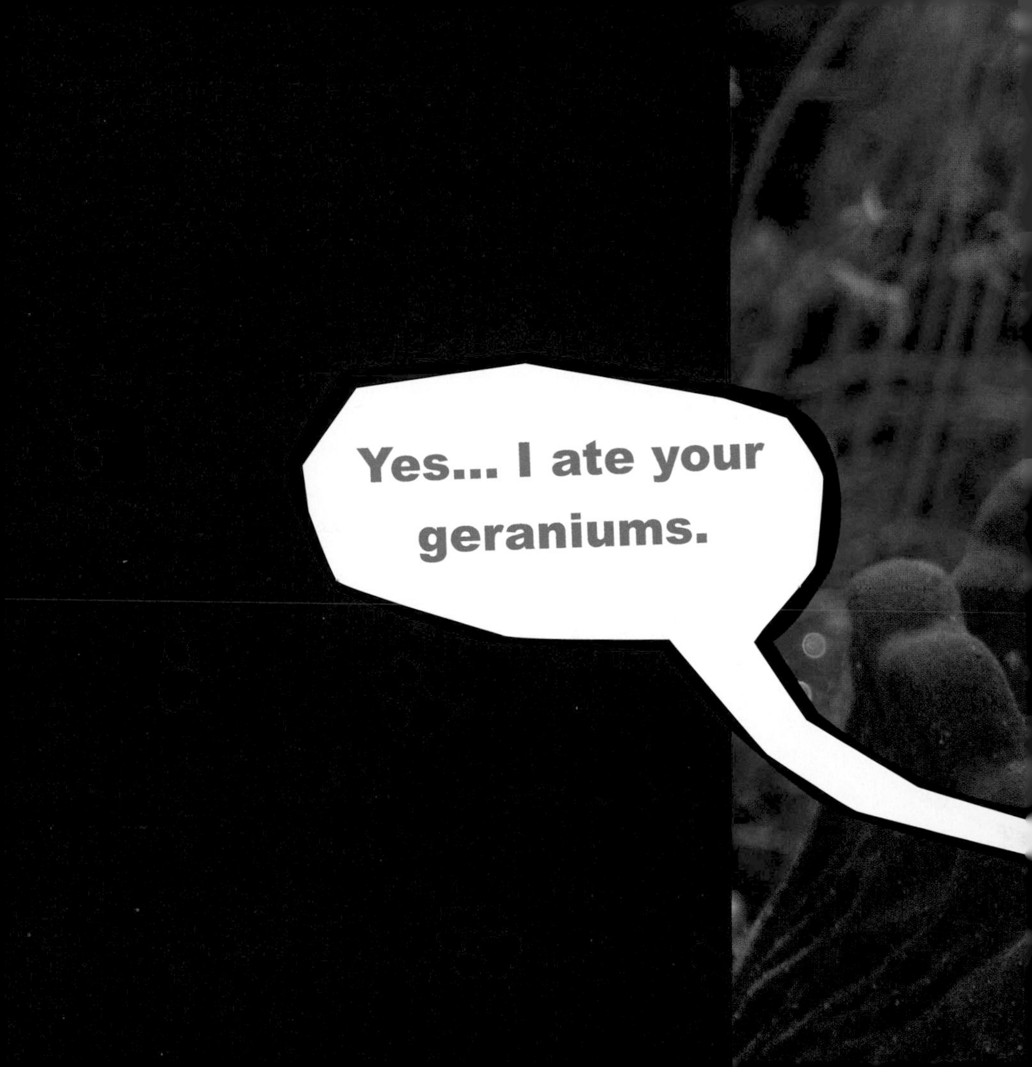
Yes... I ate your geraniums.

Only an idiot would mistake me for a gremlin. Are you an idiot? ARE YOU?

So, Mr Bond...

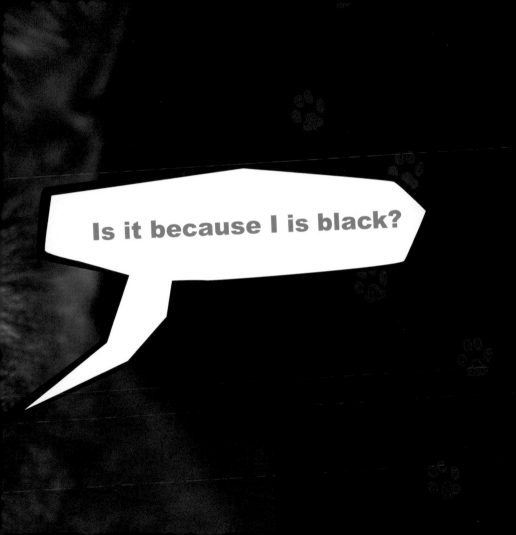

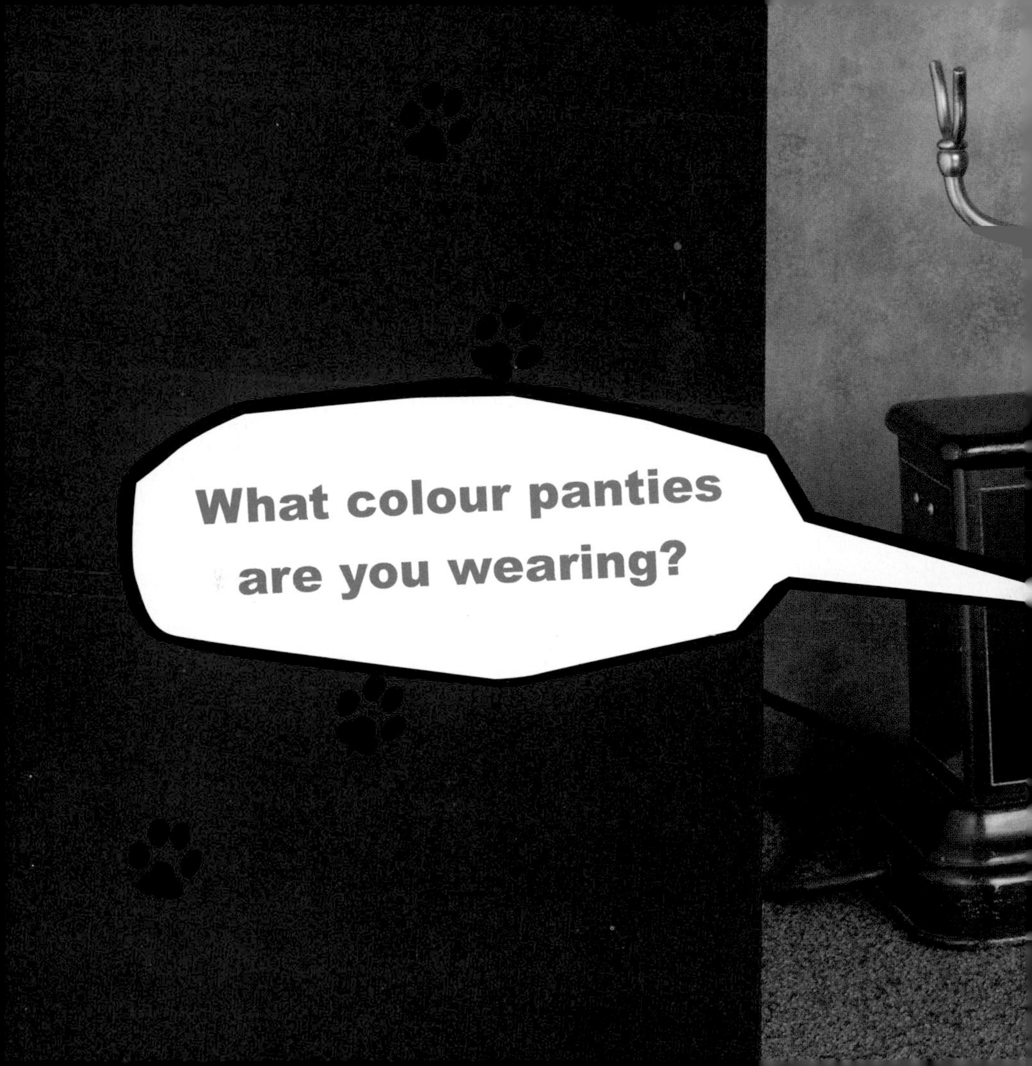
What colour panties are you wearing?

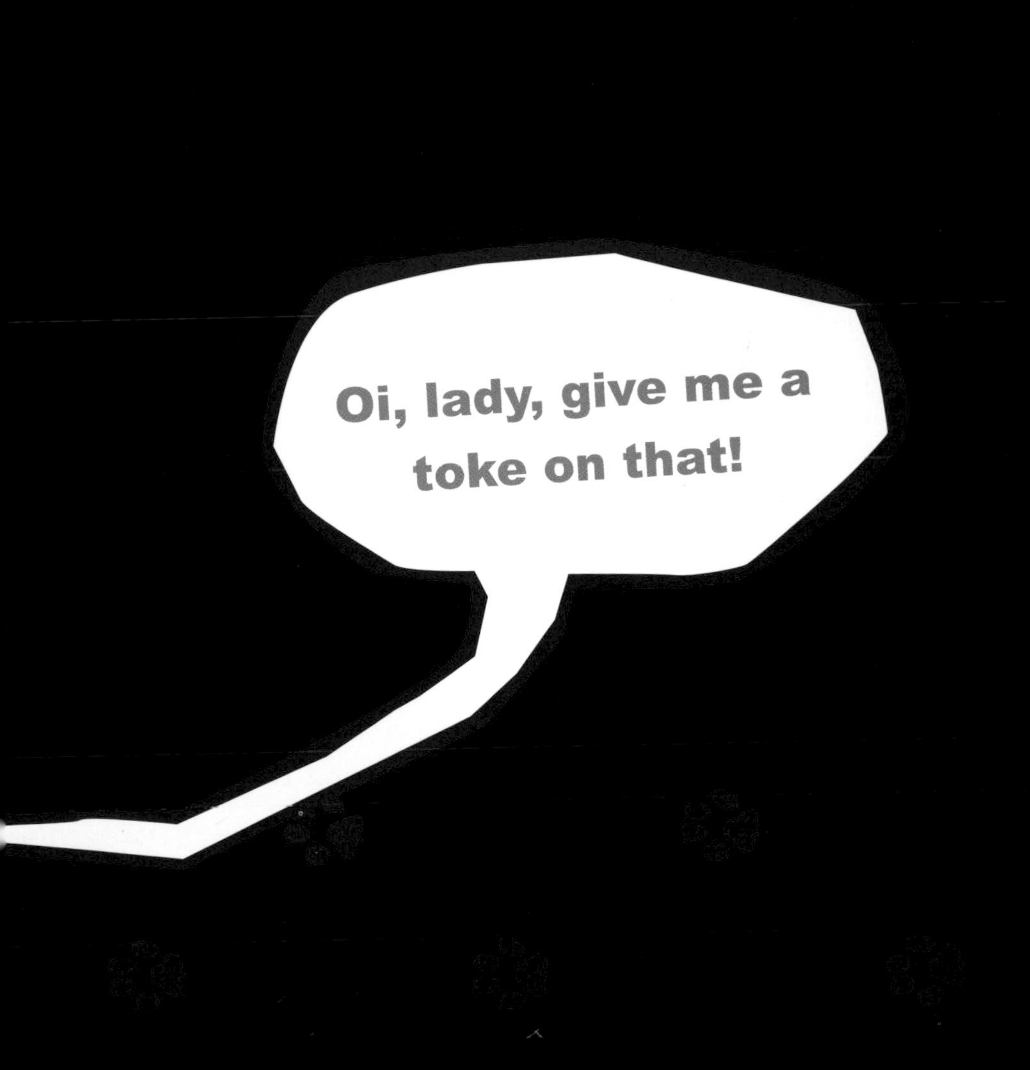
Oi, lady, give me a toke on that!

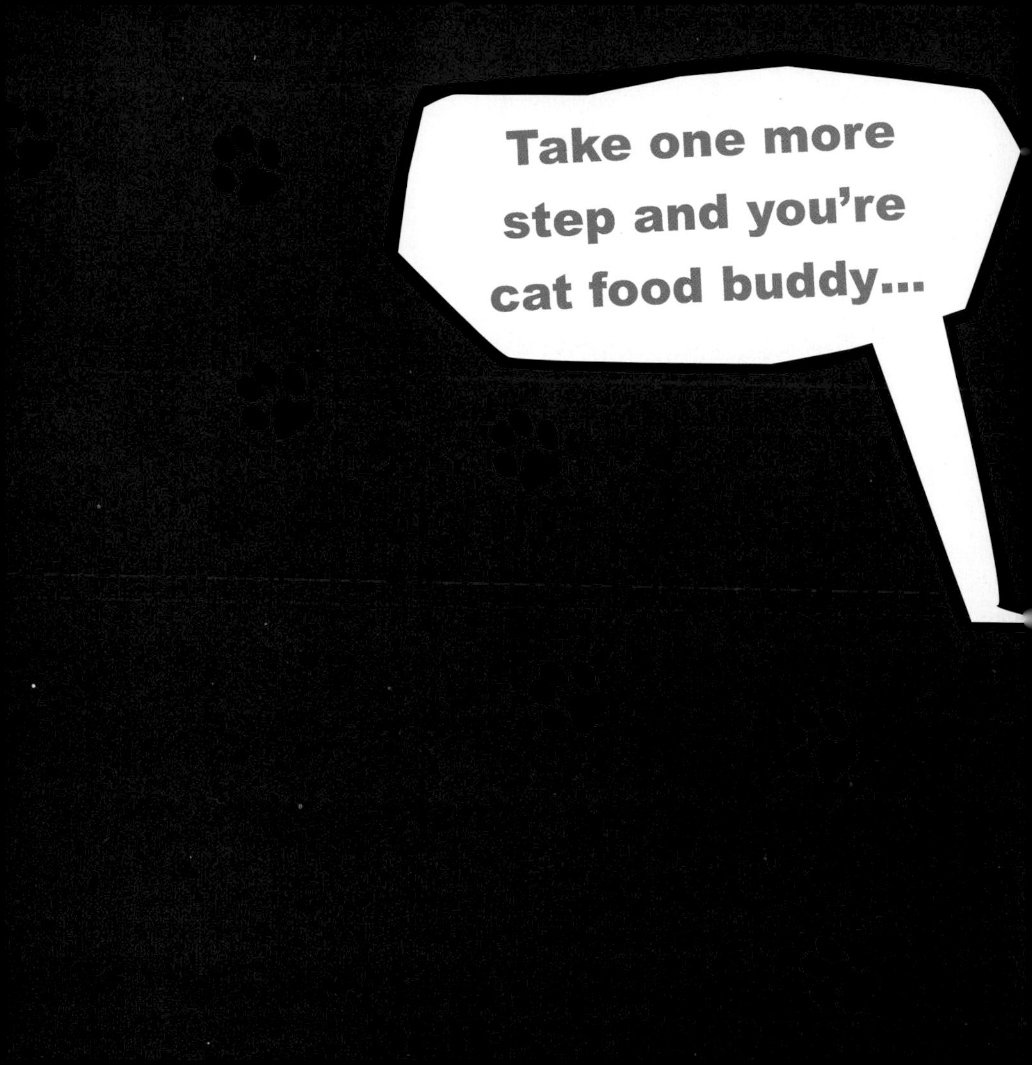
Take one more step and you're cat food buddy...

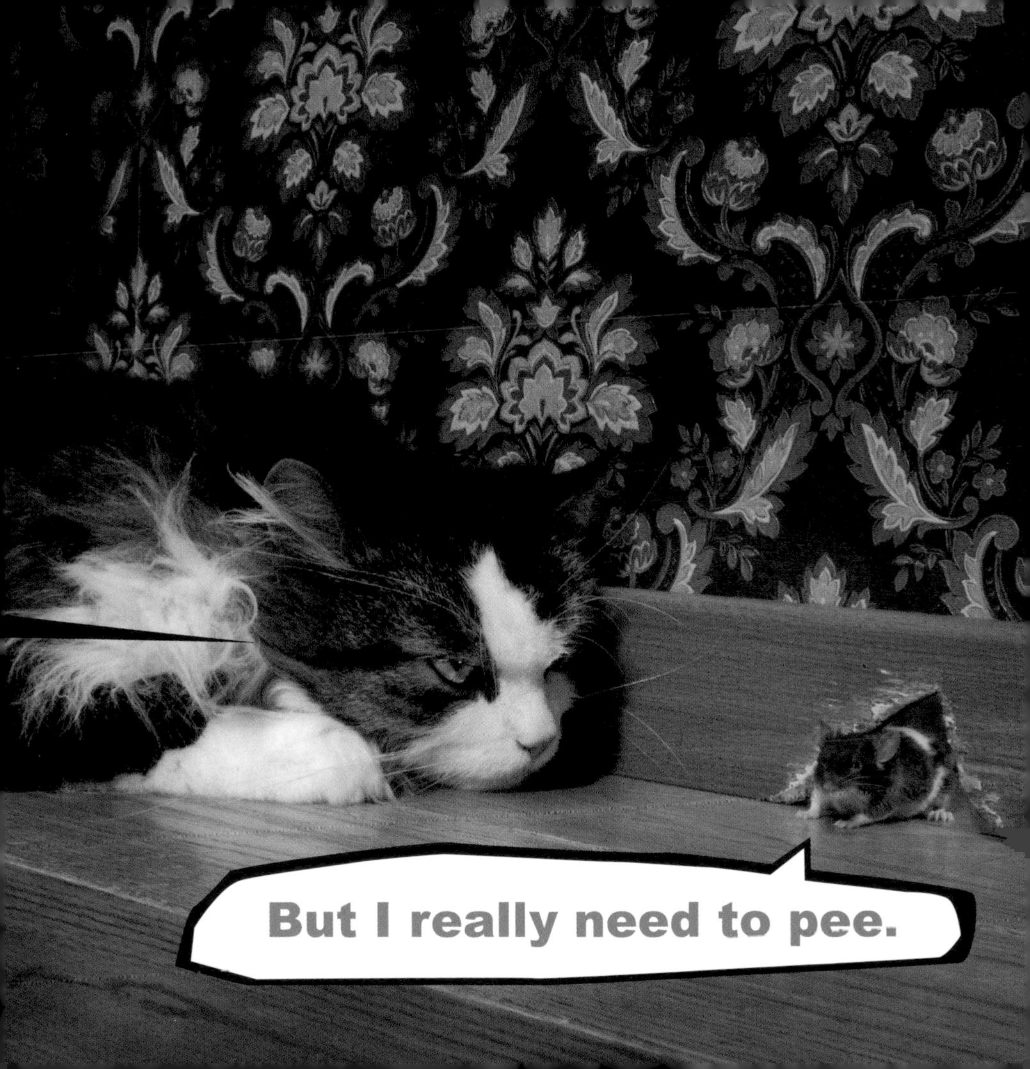
But I really need to pee.

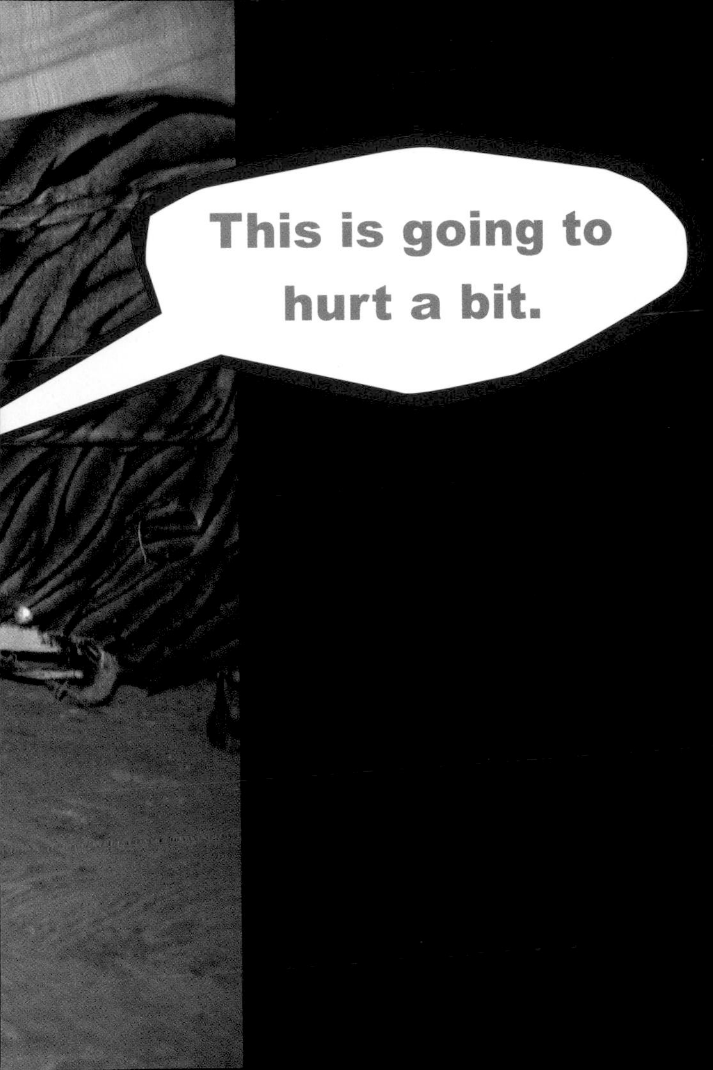
This is going to hurt a bit.

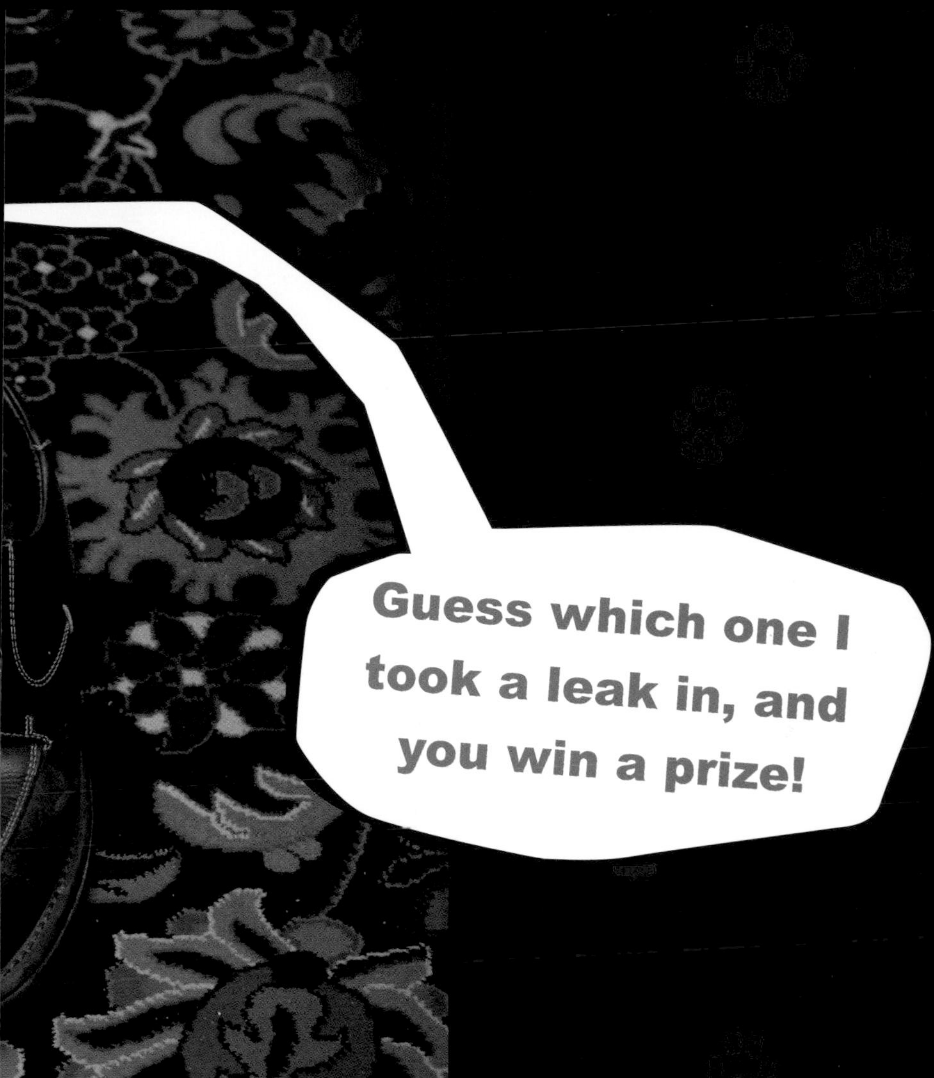
Guess which one I took a leak in, and you win a prize!

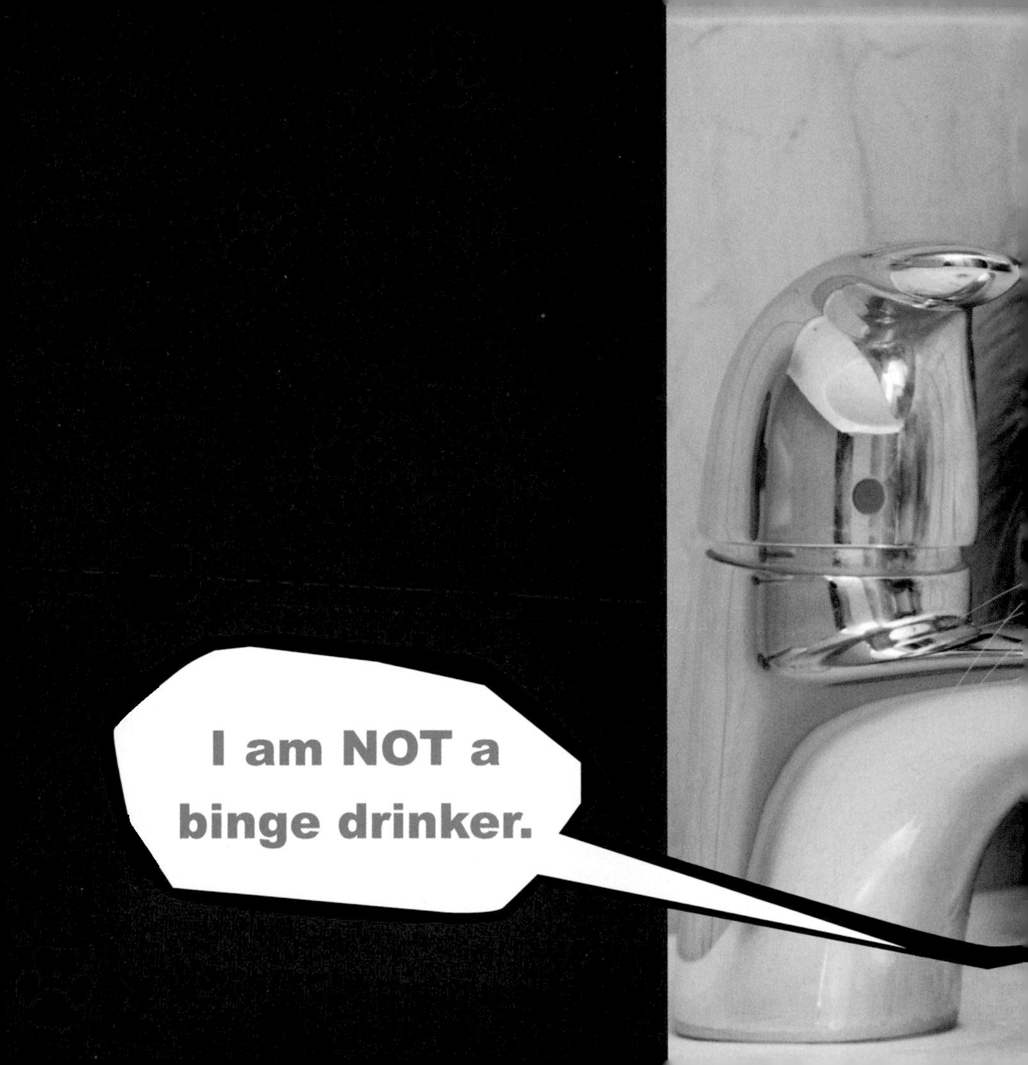
I am NOT a binge drinker.

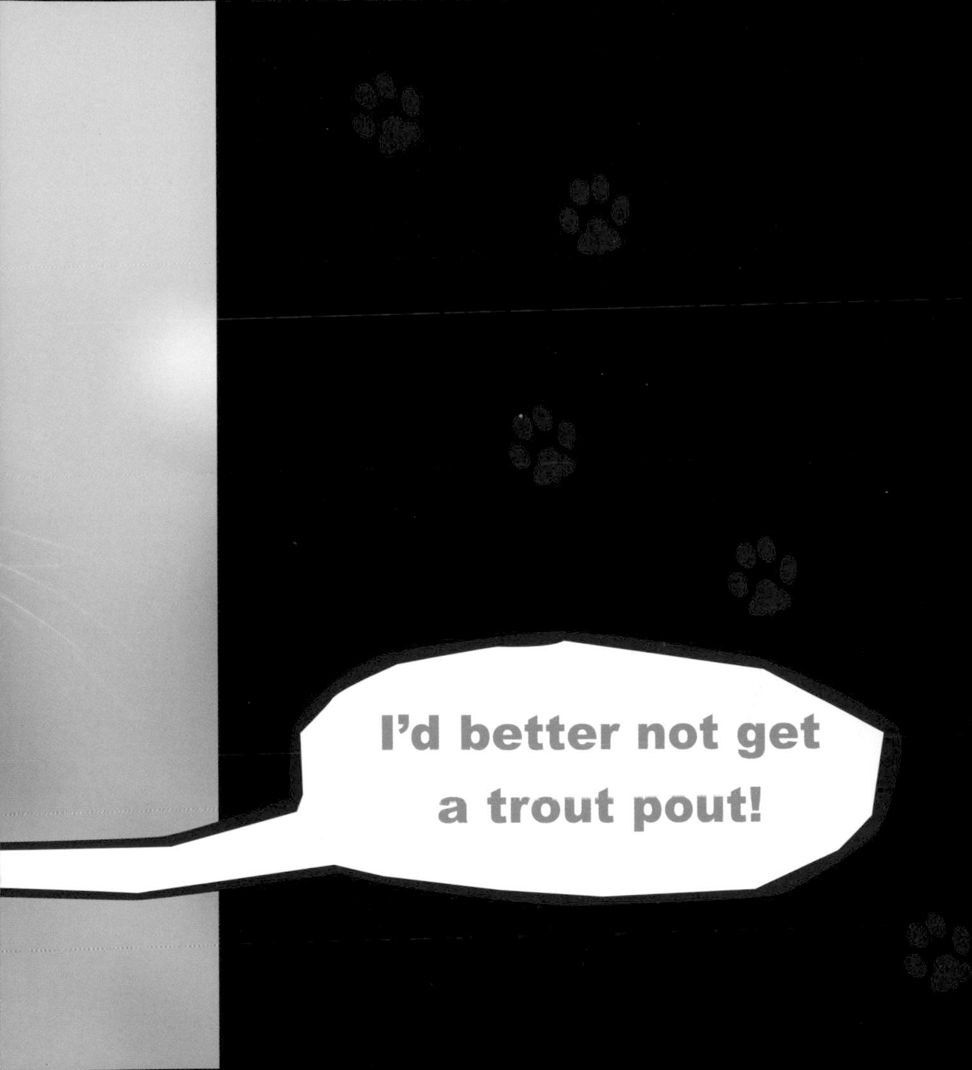
I'd better not get a trout pout!

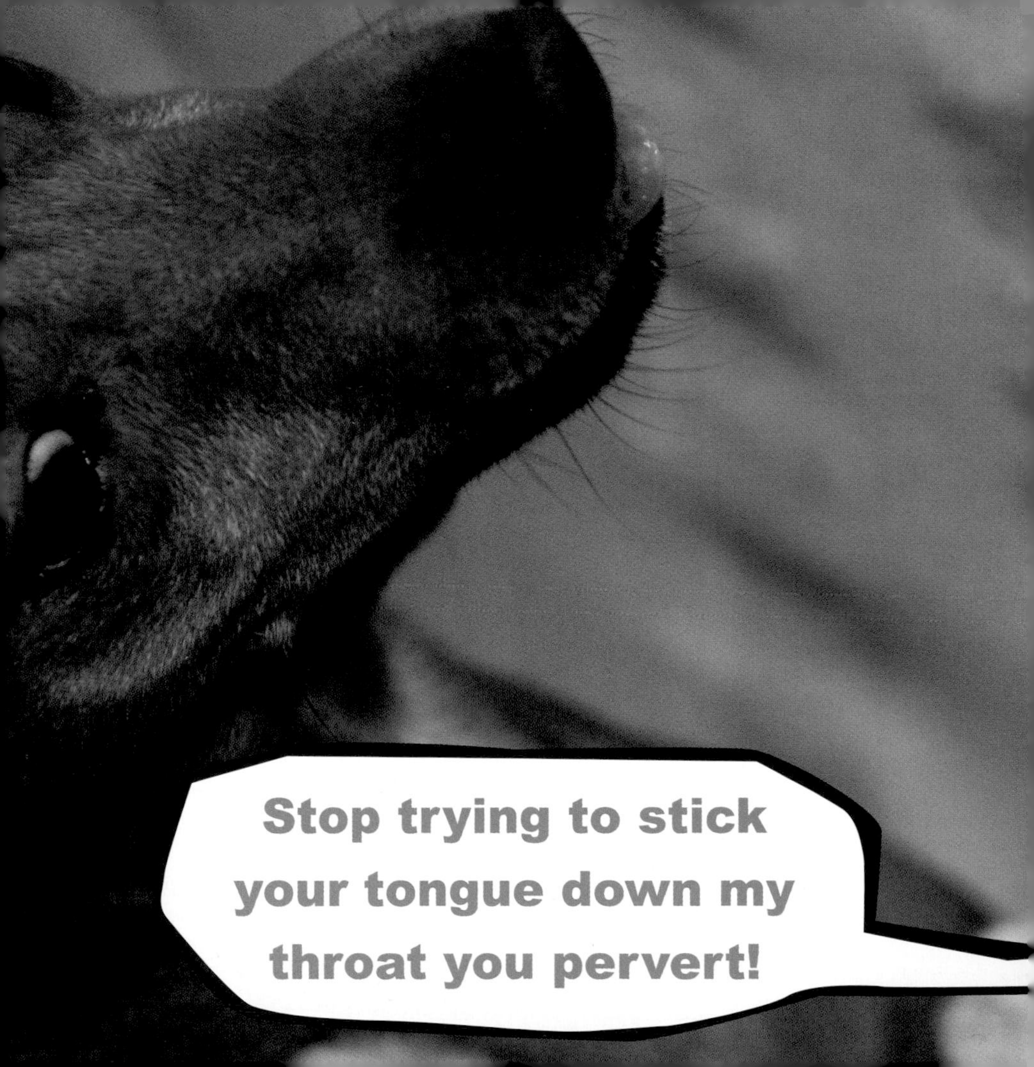
Stop trying to stick your tongue down my throat you pervert!

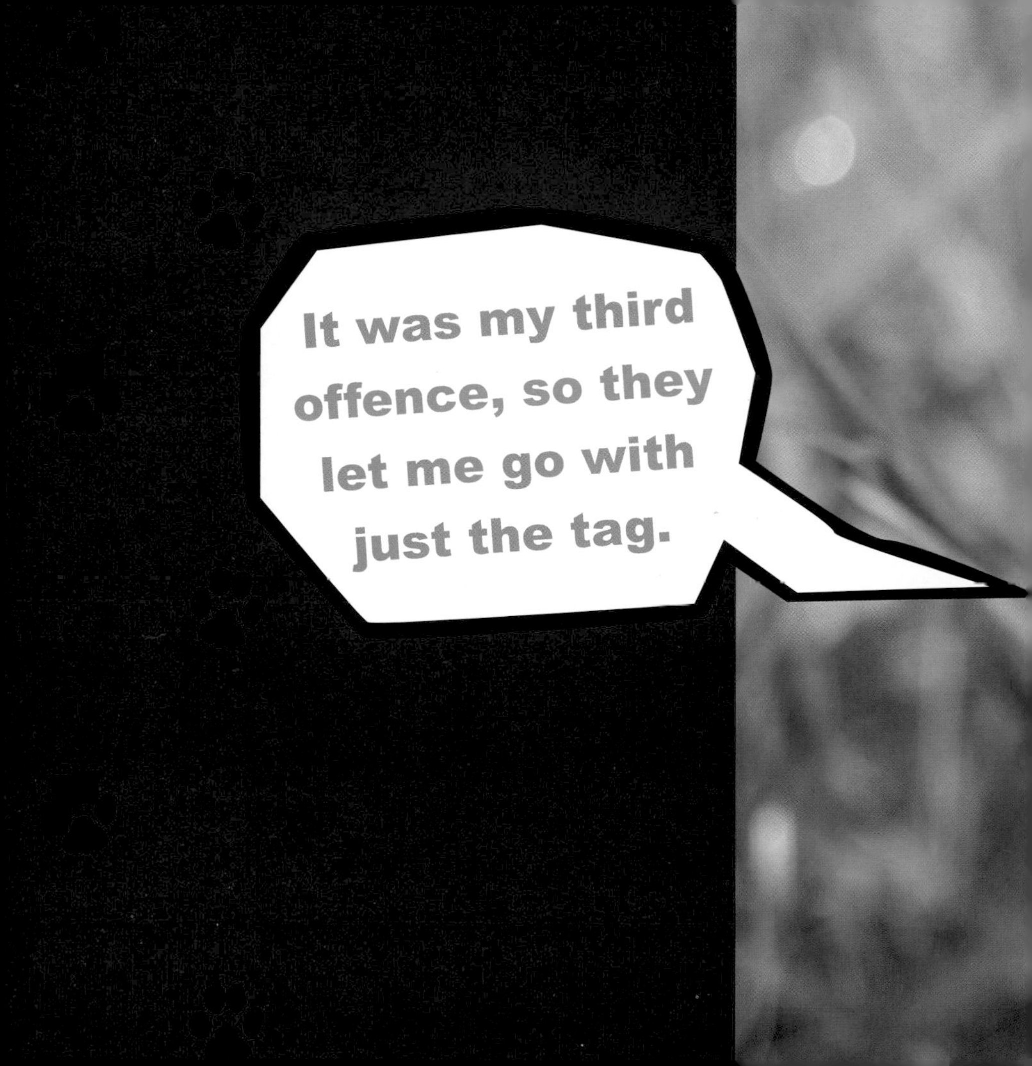
It was my third offence, so they let me go with just the tag.

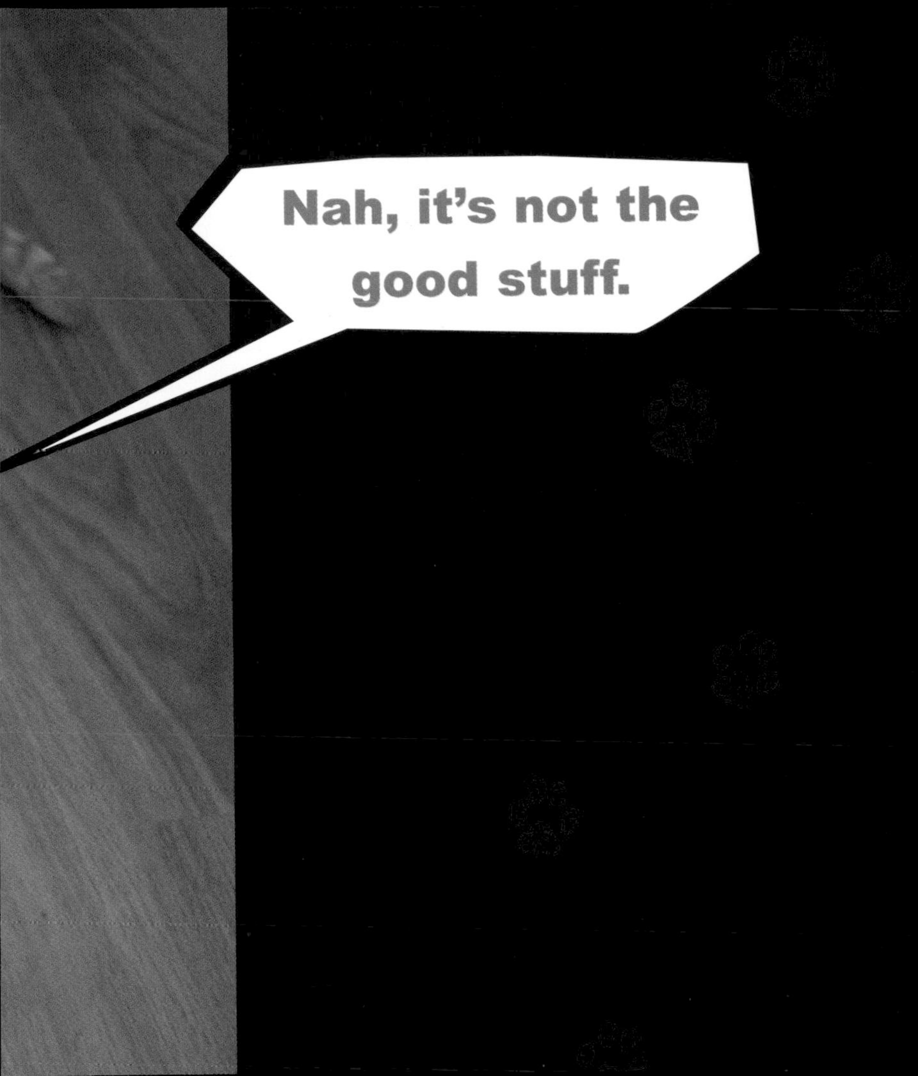
Nah, it's not the good stuff.

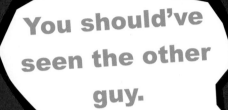

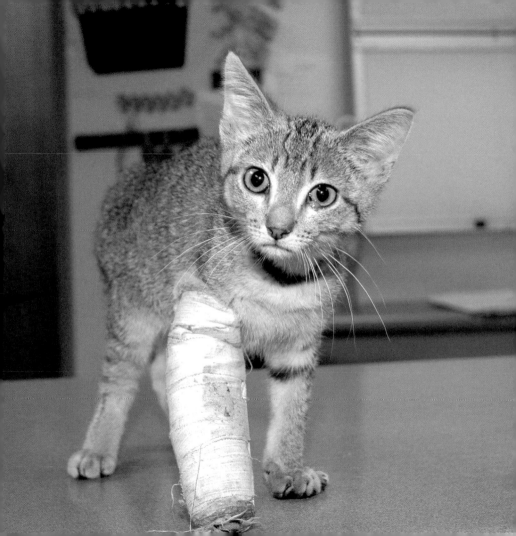

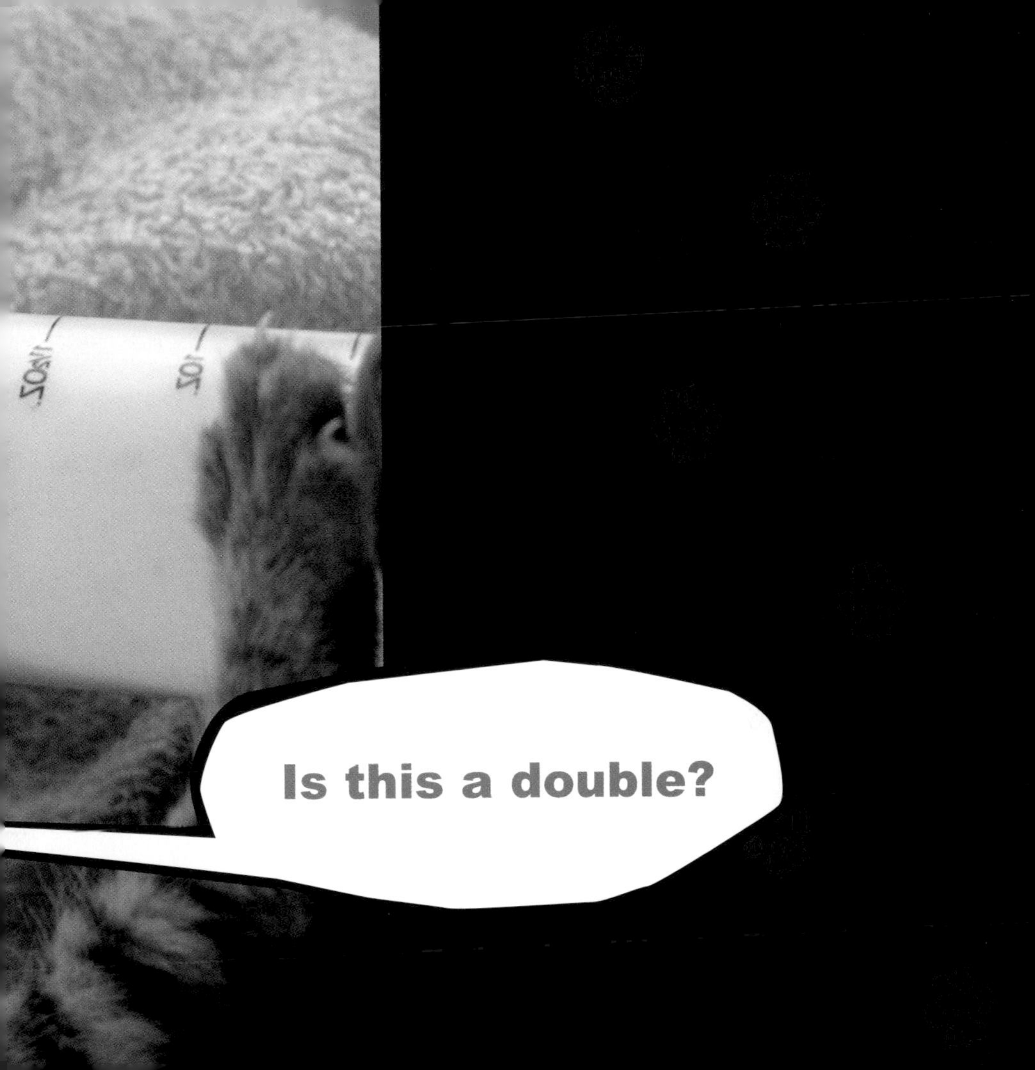
Is this a double?

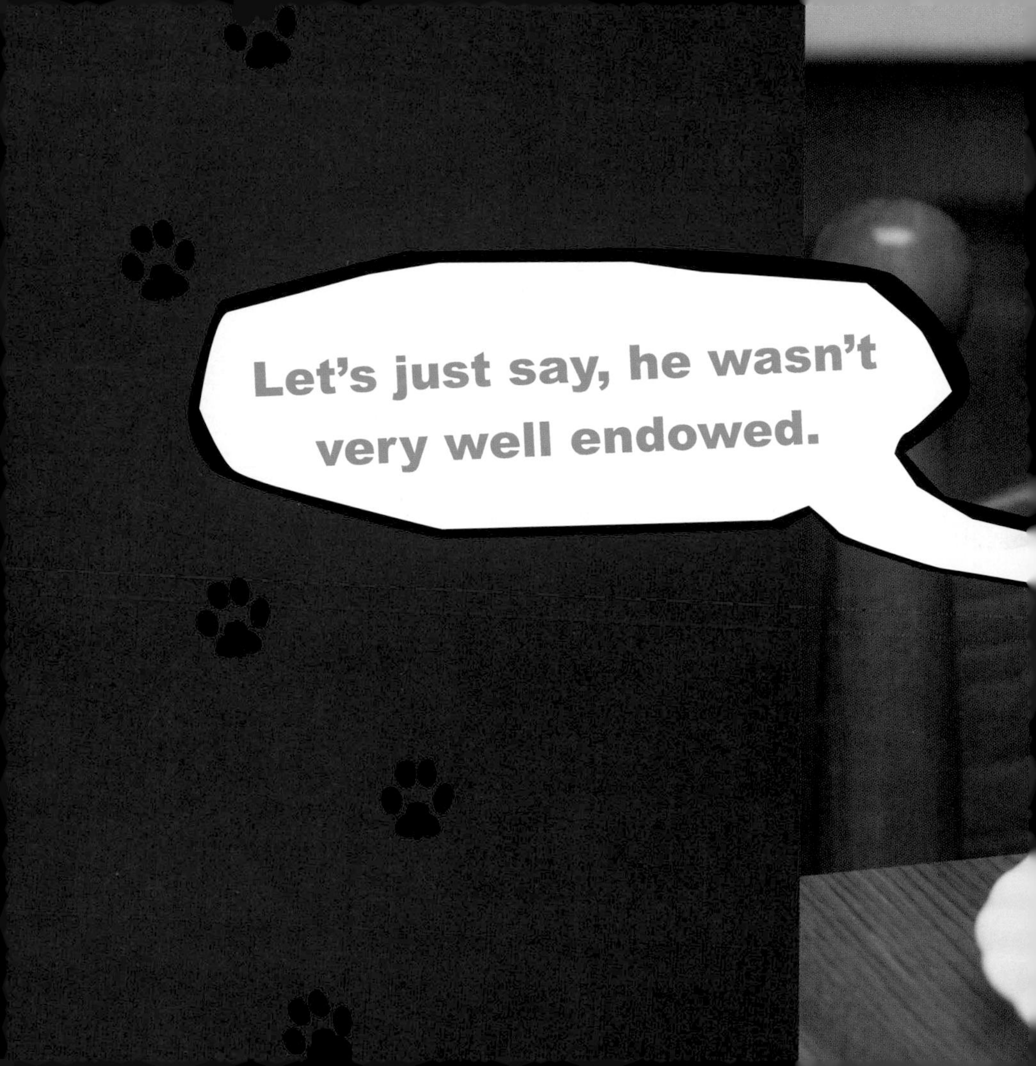
Let's just say, he wasn't very well endowed.

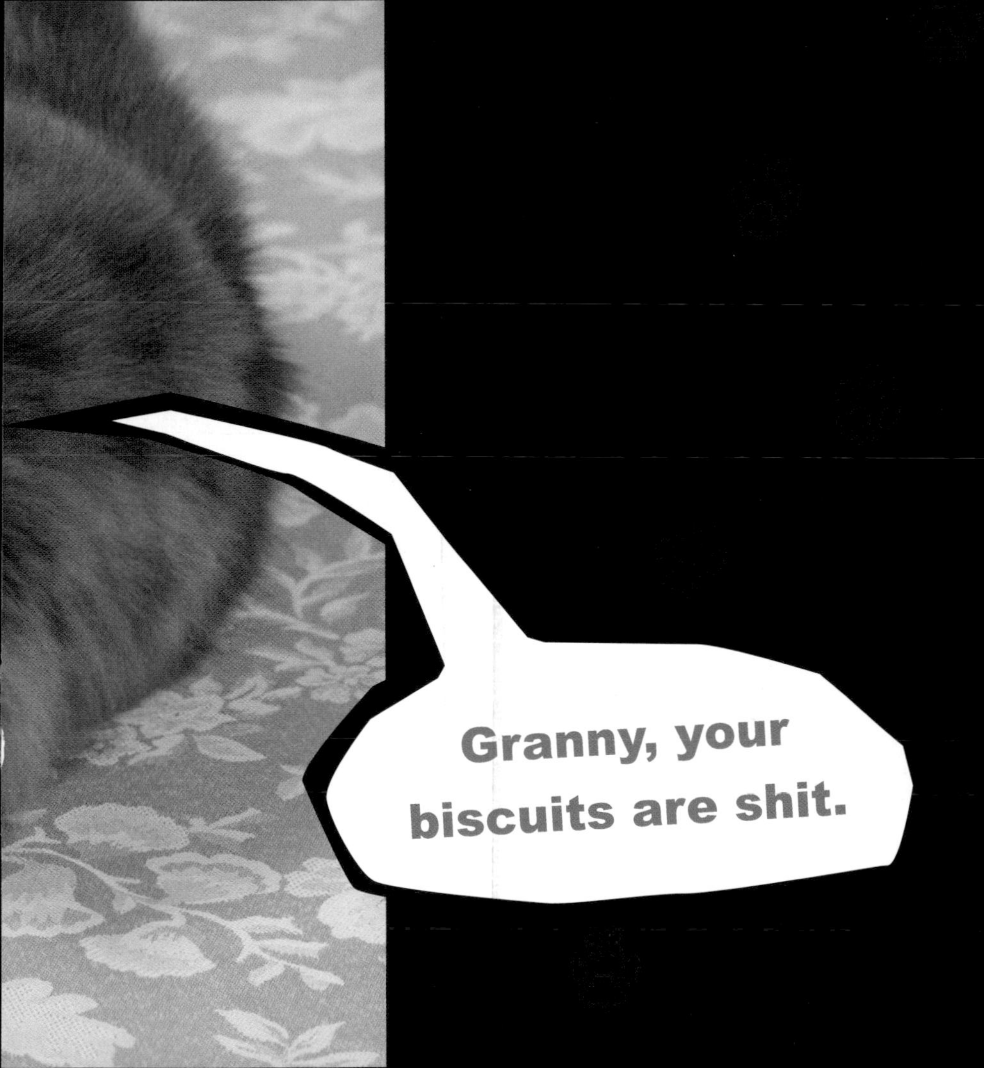
Granny, your
biscuits are shit.

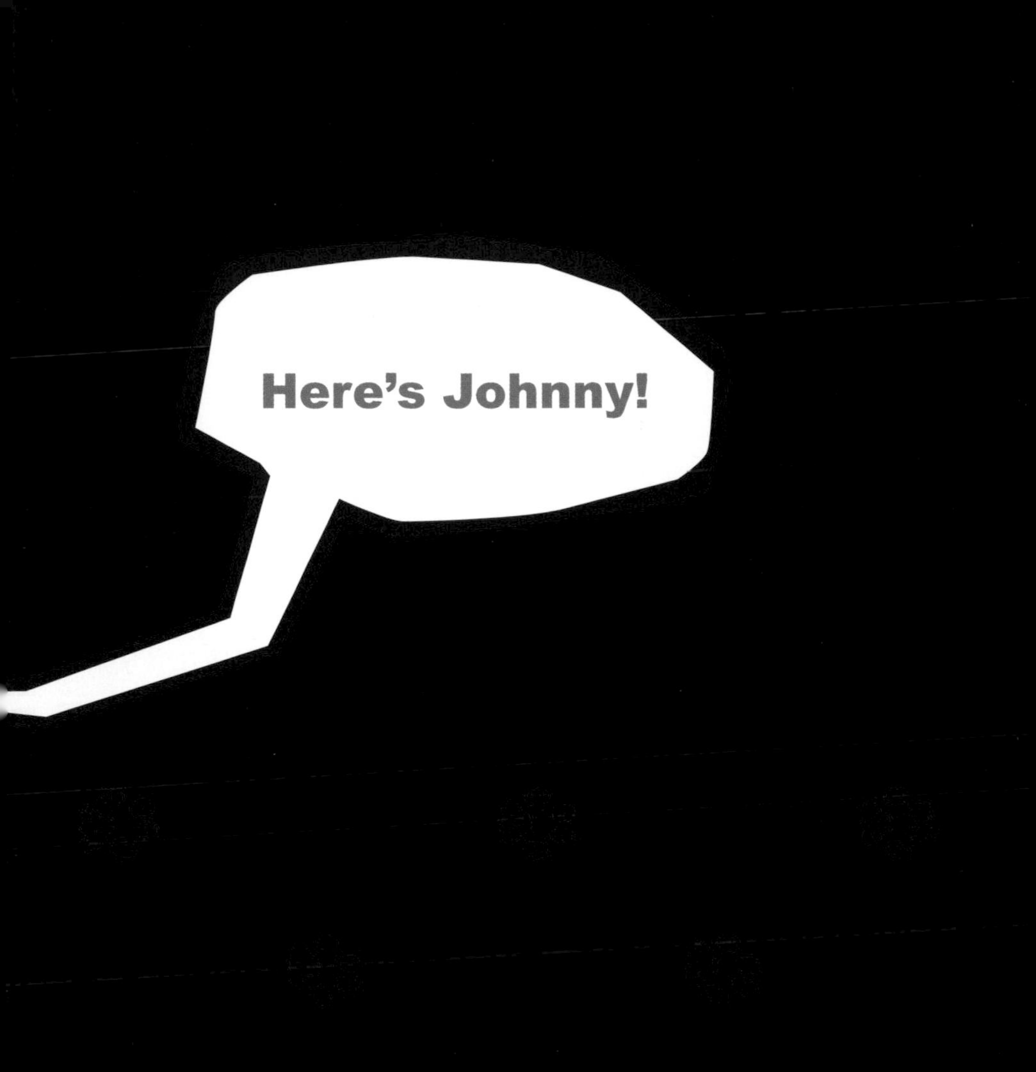
Here's Johnny!

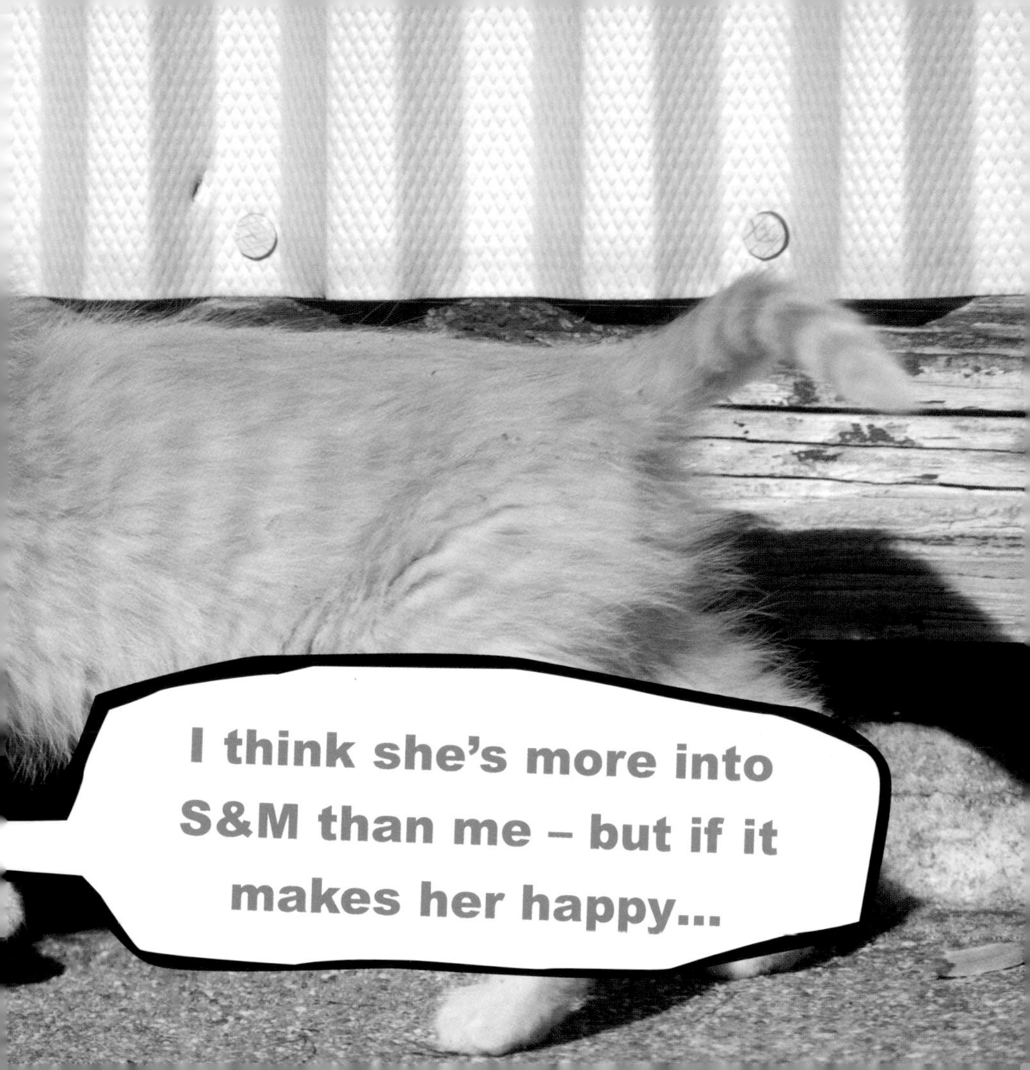
I think she's more into S&M than me – but if it makes her happy...

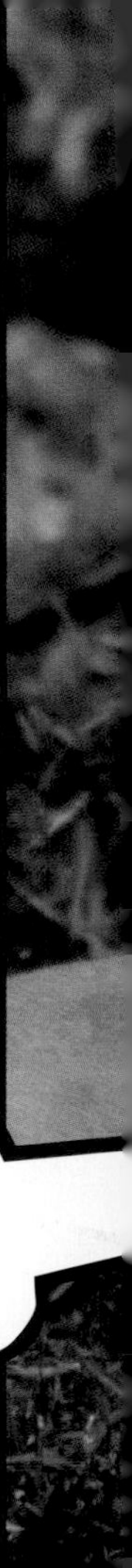

Never go down on a she-lion – you'll be removing hairs from your teeth for the next week.

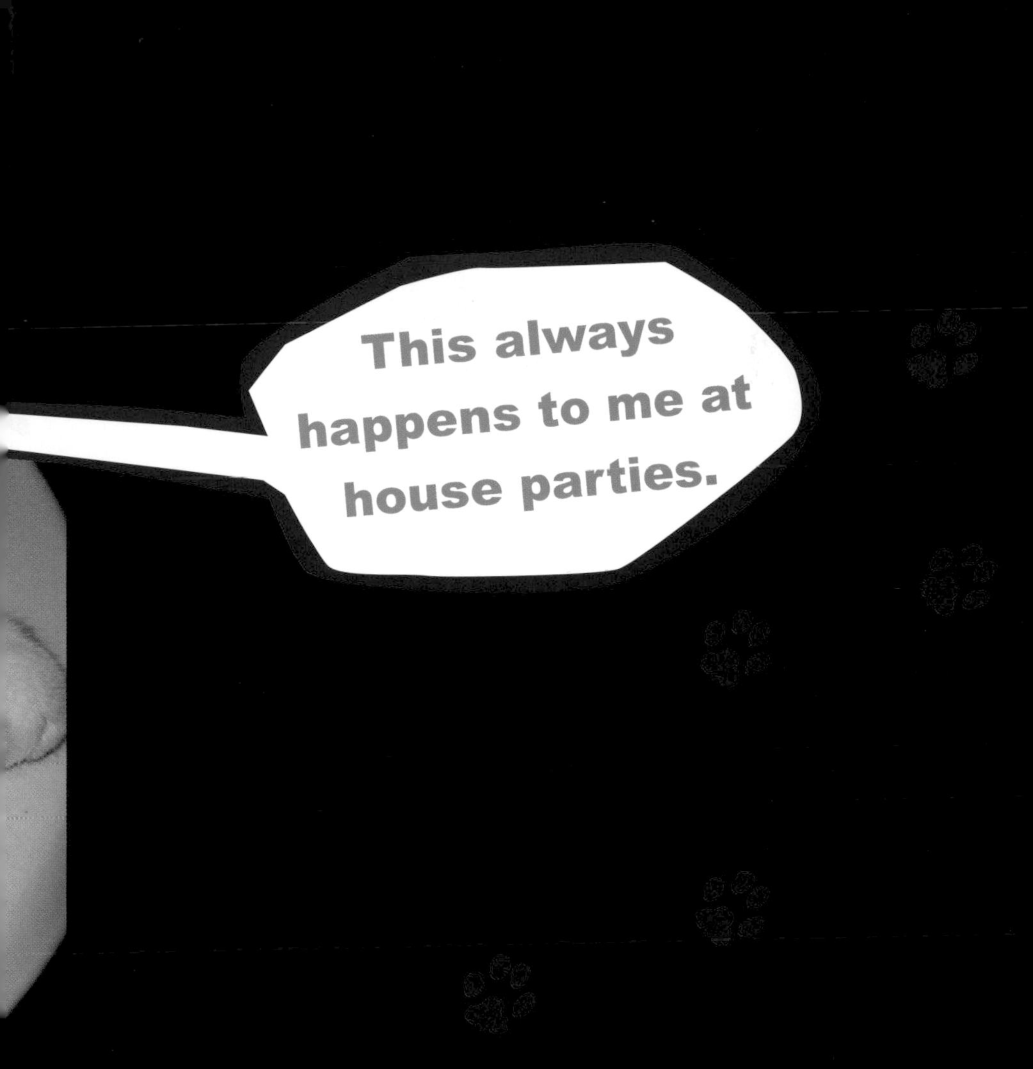
This always happens to me at house parties.

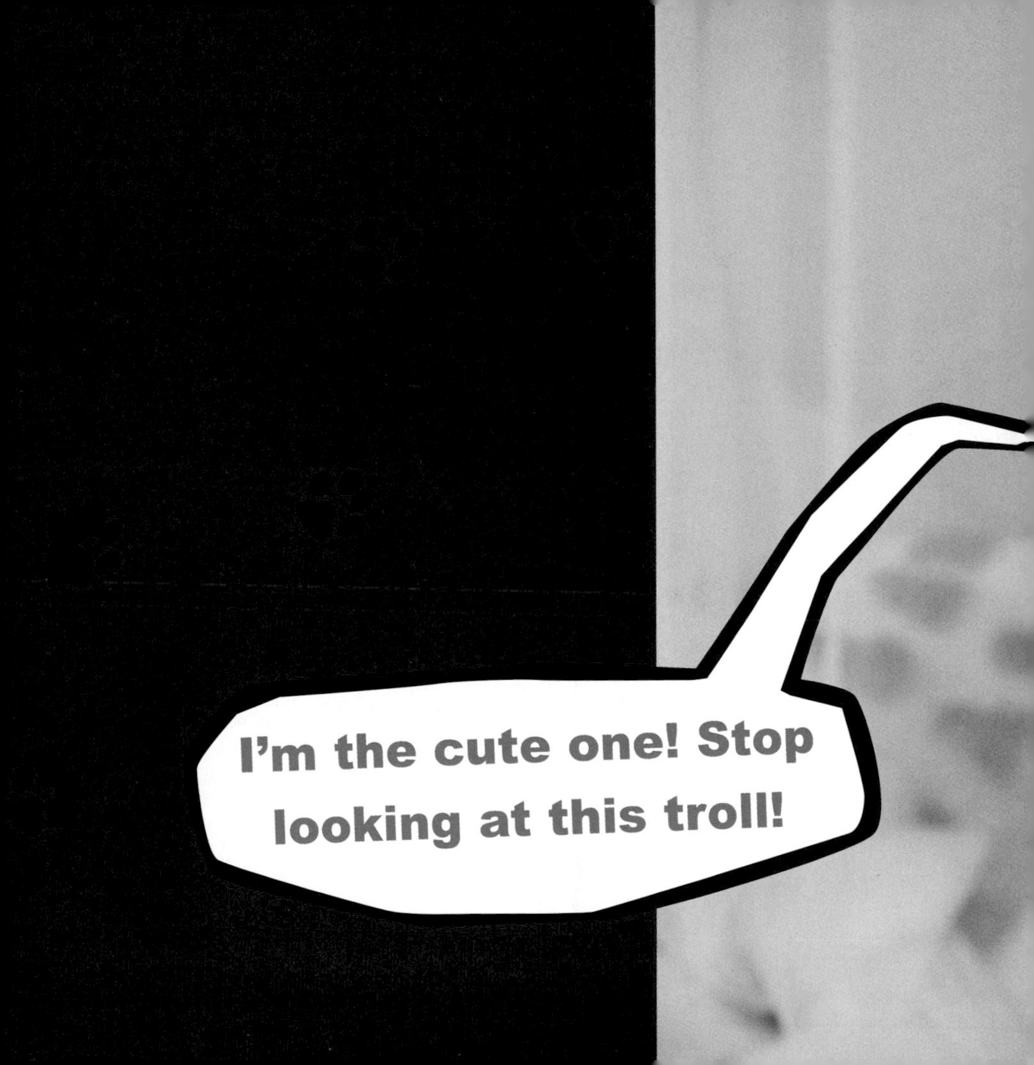
I'm the cute one! Stop looking at this troll!

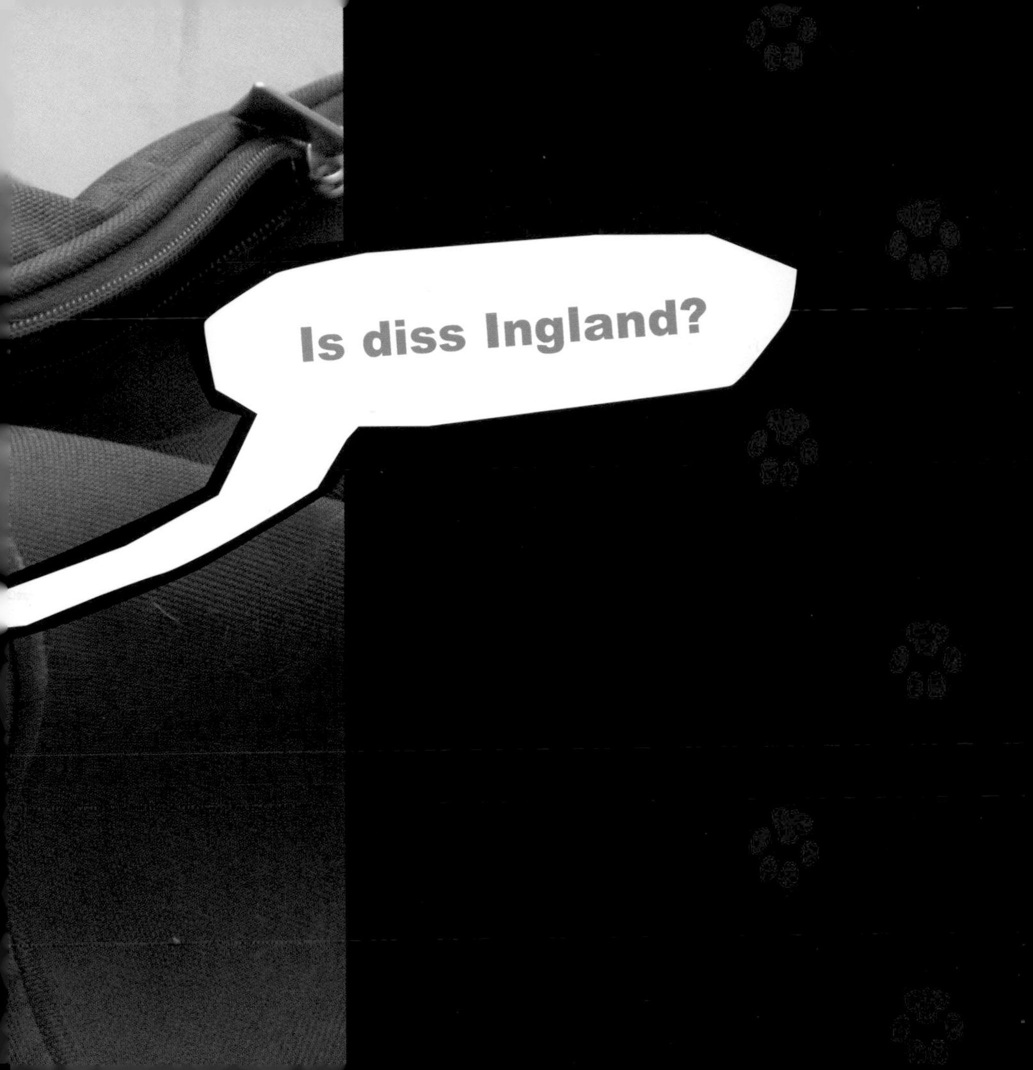
Is diss Ingland?

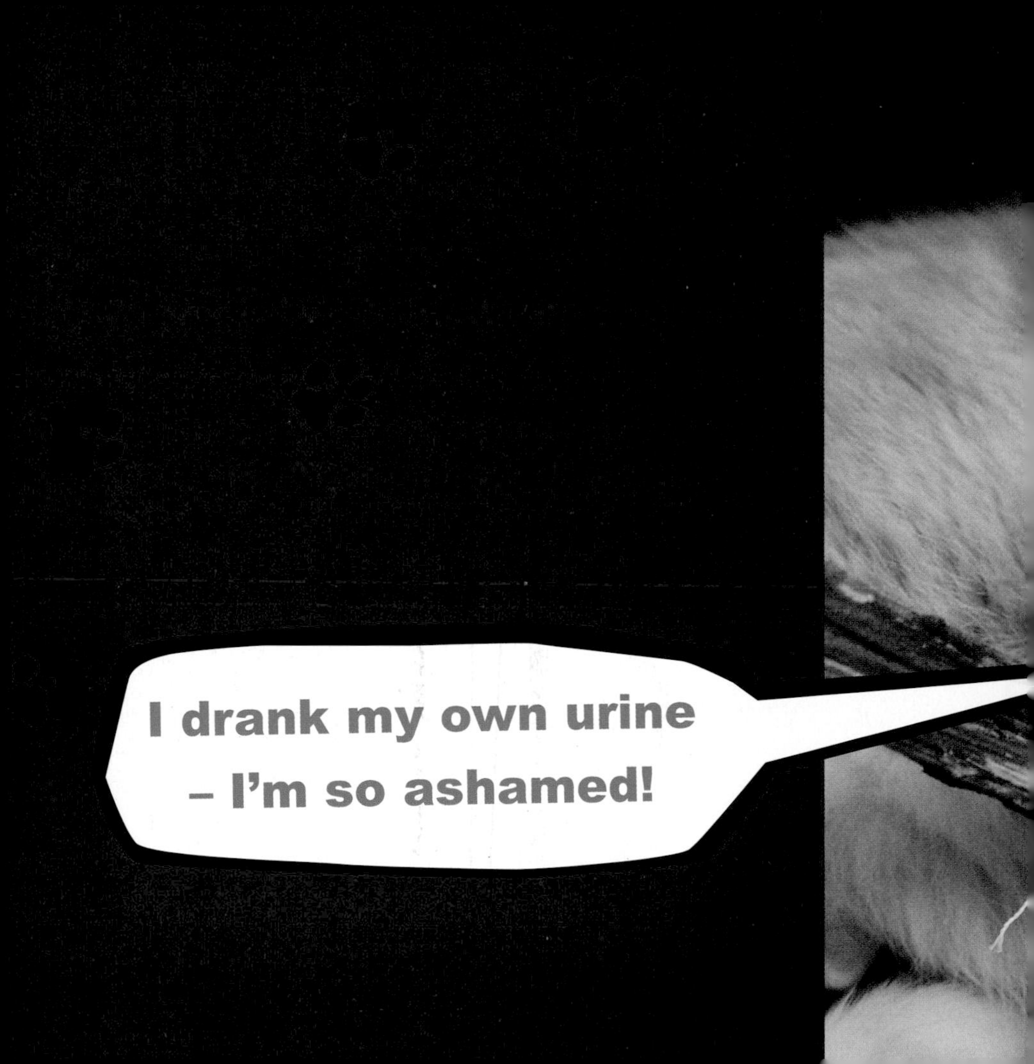
I drank my own urine – I'm so ashamed!

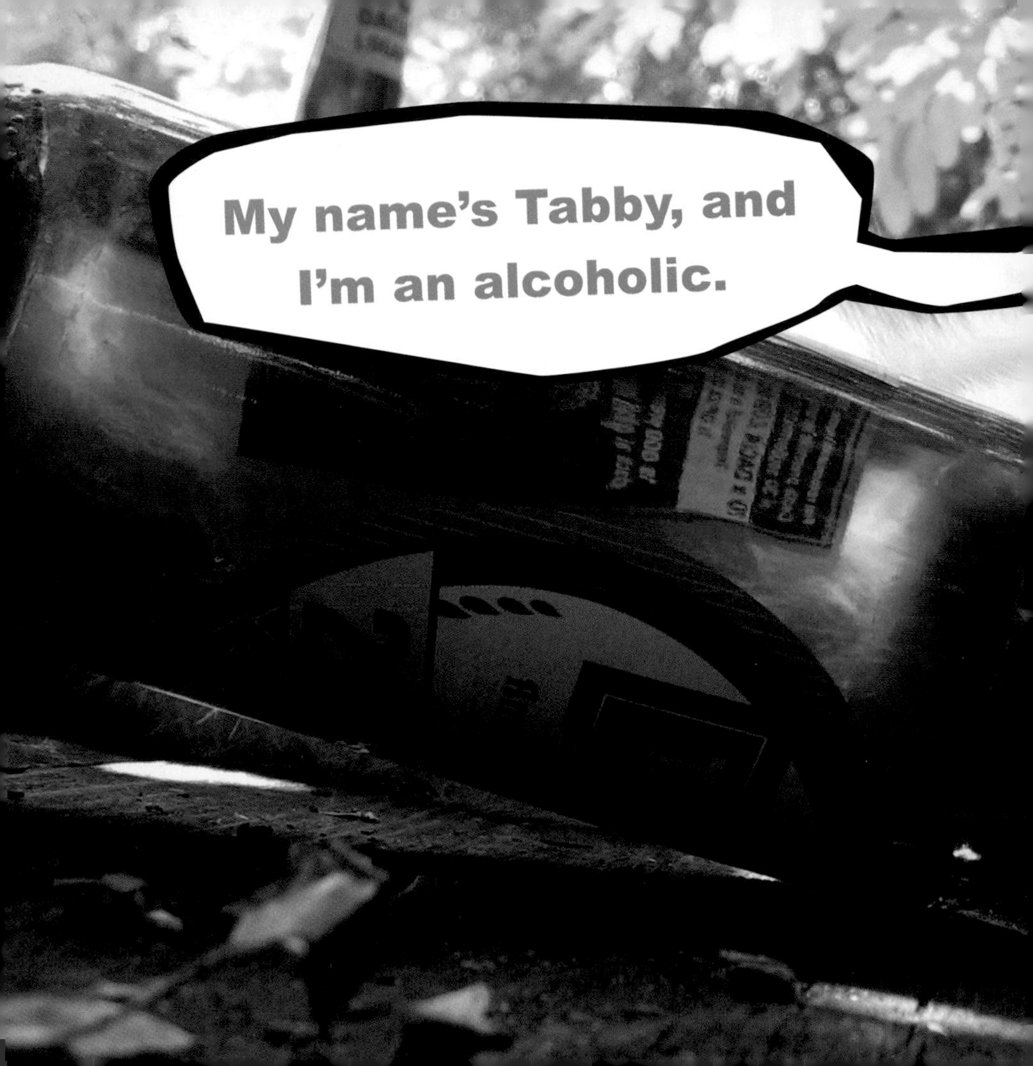
My name's Tabby, and
I'm an alcoholic.

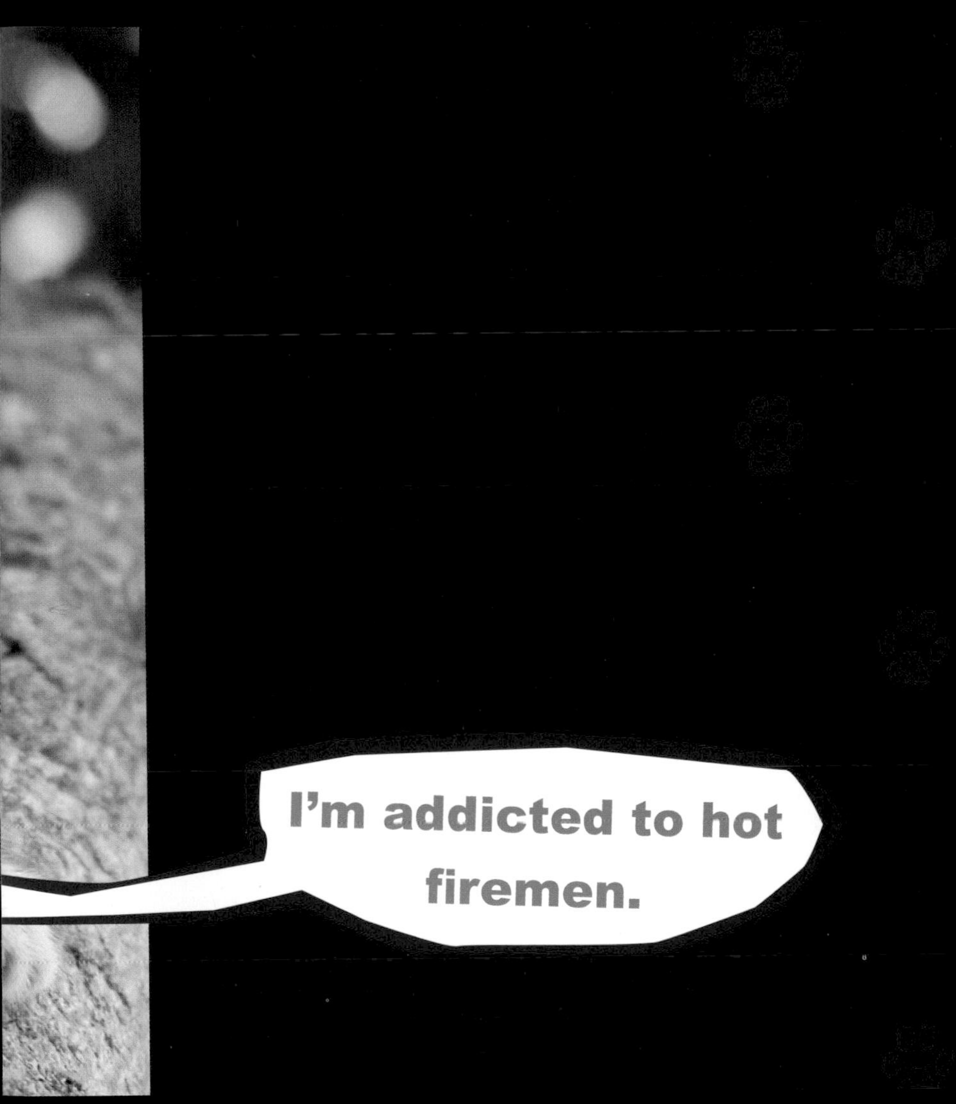
I'm addicted to hot firemen.

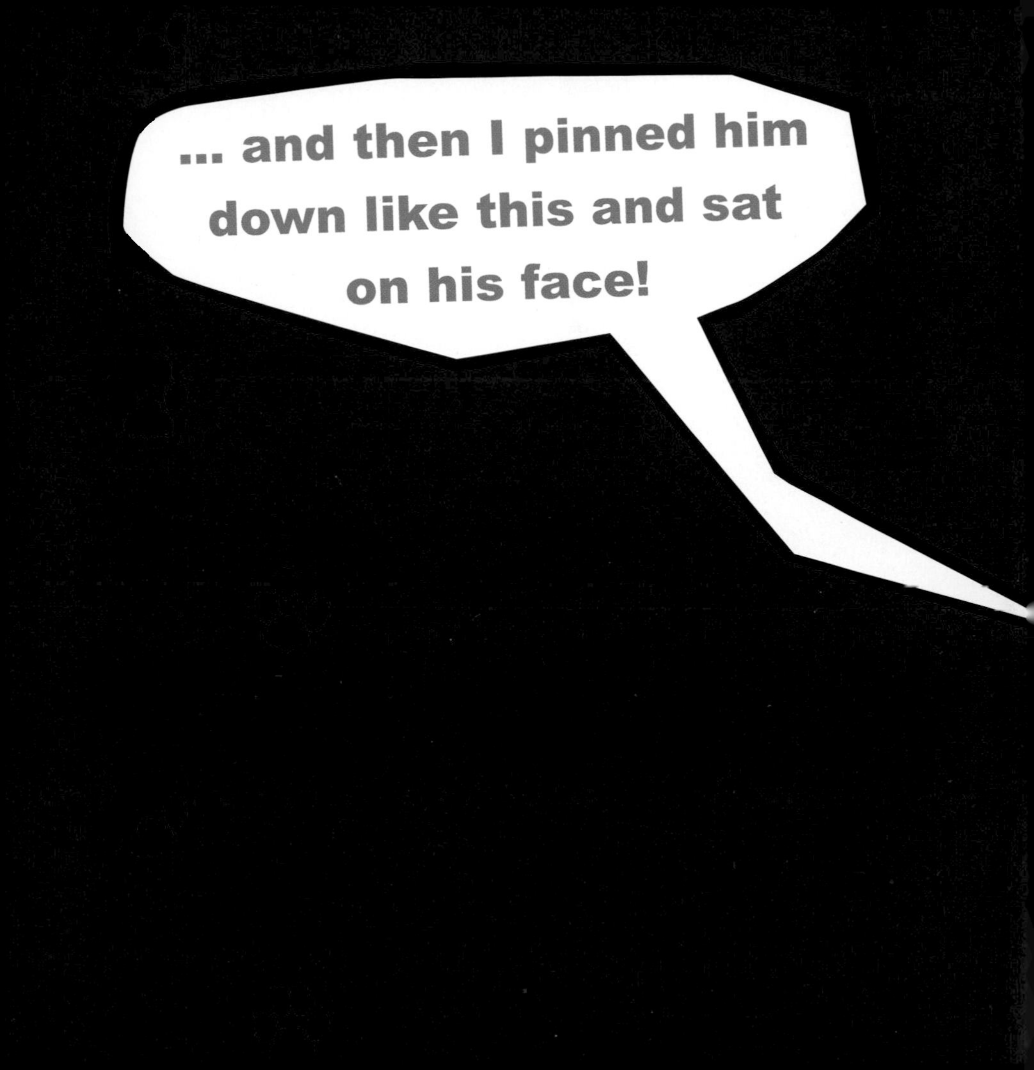
... and then I pinned him down like this and sat on his face!

Hey, Mr Brown? You've seen *Reservoir Dogs*, right? You know how this is going to go down.

PHOTO CREDITS

Have you enjoyed this book? If so, why not
write a review on your favourite website?

Thanks very much for buying
this Summersdale book.

www.summersdale.com